SHORELINE FOR THE PUBLIC

A Handbook of Social, Economic, and Legal Considerations Regarding Public Recreational Use of the Nation's Coastal Shoreline

SHORELINE FOR THE PUBLIC

A Handbook of Social, Economic, and Legal Considerations
Regarding Public Recreational Use of the Nation's Coastal
Shoreline

Dennis W. Ducsik

The MIT Press
Cambridge, Massachusetts, and London, England

245433

PUBLISHER'S NOTE

This format is intended to reduce the cost of publishing certain works in book form and to shorten the gap between editorial preparation and final publication. The time and expense of detailed editing and composition in print have been avoided by photographing the text of this book directly from the author's typescript.

The MIT Press

Report Number MITSG 74-16
Index Number 74-616-Cdp
Library of Congress catalog card number: 74-4528
ISBN 0 262 04045 X
Printed in the United States of America

TO MY FAMILY

Contents

Until very recently, public use and enjoyment of the Nation's coastal shoreline have been taken for granted. Despite the warning by the National Park Service over twenty years ago that the American coast accessible to the public was vanishing, our collective policy toward this great recreational resource has been one of benign neglect. In the meantime, a tidal wave of development--most of it to the exclusion of the general public--has engulfed the coastline. Numerous areas that were open to everyone for decades are now posted "Private Property--Keep Out," "No Trespassing--Private Beach," or "Lots For Sale." Unfortunately, these are the signs of the times along our shores, and they indicate that the American shoreline--every American's shoreline--is truly shrinking.

It is my conviction that the shores of the United States are a part of the common heritage of all the people, that they are impressed with a long-standing public interest, and that new means must be found to protect this great resource and make it available to the public. Inasmuch as the majority of outdoor recreation is centered around water, especially coastal waters, positive governmental action is urgently required to provide greater access to this important national asset. Too often in the past, land use decisions at the water's edge--whether concerning open beaches, tidal marshes, or urban waterfronts--have been made on the basis of expediency, parochial interests, and short-term economic considerations. In the absence of both foresight and adequate resources in the public sector, diffusely-held public concerns have been left by default to the unilateral decisionmaking processes of private developers. If the American people are to avoid forfeiting completely their heritage in and claim to the seacoast, the institutional ar-

rangements and decisionmaking processes which determine allocation among competing uses must be carefully reevaluated.

The balanced use of shorelands as between the needs for
public recreation and the demands for private development is
an important element affecting the quality of the coastal
environment. This book lays the groundwork for the development of effective policies to combat the continuing encroachment on the public interest in the shoreline, and to
bring about a more effective representation of that interest
in coastal decisionmaking. It provides a coordinated statement of the dimensions of the problem, the techniques that
are available to deal with it, and the challenges that lie
ahead. What is needed now is the desire to press forward
with the task.

I am pleased that Mr. Ducsik's work is an outgrowth of a
previous association with the United States Senate Committee
on Interior and Insular Affairs, on which I serve as
chairman.

I firmly believe that, in the activities of Congressional
committees, there are many occasions where scholarly and
in-depth research, analysis, and innovative thought by persons trained in a wide variety of disciplines and unshackled
by institutional attitudes and conventional wisdom could be
of immeasureable assistance. The Committee's professional
staff can, of course, give only limited time and bring a few
disciplines--law, engineering, public administration--to a
particular study.

On January 29, 1970, I introduced in the United States
Senate the first national land use policy bill. When this
measure was referred to the Interior Committee, I felt that
professors and advanced students in the many disciplines as-

sociated with land use decisionmaking could render valuable
assistance to the Committee as it undertook the task of
formulating its thoughts on land use policy and evaluating
the legislative proposal. As a result, the Committee
entered into a unique Congressional-university association
with a multi-disciplinary group from the Boston area, led by
Professor Carroll L. Wilson of the Massachusetts Institute
of Technoloby. In the spring of 1970, the National Land Use
Policy Project was established, involving professors and
students from M.I.T., Woods Hole Oceangraphic Institution,
Boston University, and Tufts University. The participant's
backgrounds included: urban planing, ecology, civil engineering, electrical engineering, management, operations
research, political science, and law. The students received
academic credit for their work and several of their papers
were published by the Interior Committee in a print entitled
Papers on National Land Use Policy Issues. Mr. Ducsik's
paper on recreational use of the Nation's shoreline, included in that print, was the precursor of this book.

Most assuredly, just as with Mr. Ducsik's earlier effort
on shoreline management, this lengthier, more comprehensive
work will enter the public realm and contribute to national
policy-making. To anyone concerned about our Nation's
vanishing shoreline, and to anyone charged with the task of
protecting it, I commend this insightful book.

May 7, 1974   Henry M. Jackson
Washington, D.C.   United States Senator

It is often said that the integral relationship between man and the natural environment is best exemplified by his long and close association with the sea, and nowhere is this association more acutely manifest than at the seashore itself. The tactile sensations of the land-sea interface allow man the unique and perhaps unparalleled experience of communion with the marine environment, which for so long has helped sustain him. So valued has been this opportunity, so clear has been the importance of having all men share equally in it, that even in ancient Roman times the shoreline was recognized as properly "the common property of all."

Unfortunately, in the United States at least, such observations can only be considered now as allusions to the romantic past. The Scottish essayist, Thomas Carlyle, once warned a land-rich 19th century America that when population outstripped these resources our trials would begin, and his prediction has come true as far as the coastal shoreline is concerned. With ever-rising affluence, we have found that more and more individuals can afford to reserve for themselves a part of what was formerly the common heritage of everyone. As a result, the waterfront lot has replaced the public beach as the modern symbol of coastal America. And the concept of shoreline for the public has become more an elusive dream than a cherished tradition.

There is evidence, however, that the tide is beginning to turn in favor of reclaiming the public interest in the shoreline. This is part of a larger trend witnessed in recent years, the emergence of our industrial society from the 'dark ages' of degradation and abuse of the natural environment. Anthony Wolff, the writer, has said that "we are turned back upon ourselves, a prodigal nation newly poor in unspoiled places, looking for last resorts where we can revive ourselves" -- and this revival has begun to reach the seashore. An upwelling of concern for increased public access to the coast has materialized at all levels of society, from the 'grass roots' to the state courts and legislatures and finally to the Congress of the United States. In Connecticut, a man named Ned Coll has been waging a one-man battle to get the urban poor onto beaches heretofore reserved exclusively for residents of the coastal suburbs. In Massachusetts, support is growing for proposals to make beach-walking legal and to reassert public control of shoreline rights-of-way. In New Jersey, Florida, Texas, California, and Oregon, judges have affirmed rights of the public at large to use and have access to seashores. And in the nation's capital, the Congress is considering legislation to protect the public interest in open beaches on a nationwide basis.

This book exists to add but another voice to the growing chorus of concern for the public interest in the nation's shores. Its objectives are twofold: to develop an understanding of the nature of the problem of decreasing coastal open space for public use, and its causal factors; and to set forth the tools of public policy that can be used to halt and reverse this trend. The question of how much seashore should ultimately be devoted to public use is not at issue, for this will be a function of the evolution of social values over time, and can only be answered by the body politic. On the other hand, it can and should be argued that more is needed, and that steps must be taken to provide it. Though a complete return to the concept of shoreline for the public will never be feasible or desirable, the time is long past when we can afford to look at the coastal situation and be willing to grin and bear it.

Thanks are due to many people in connection with the preparation of this report, especially Dean A. Horn of the MIT Sea Grant Program, William C. Brewer of the National Oceanic and Atmospheric Administration, and Ava Adams and Mary Folan of the Chandler School. Most of all, I am indebted to my patient wife, Sharon, whose gracious companionship sustained me throughout this effort.

Cambridge, Massachusetts   Dennis W. Ducsik
January 26, 1974

"Et quidem naturali jure communia sunt omnium haec, aer, aqua profundus, et mare et per hoc littora maris" -- By natural law itself these things are the common property of all: air, running water, the sea, and with it the shores of the sea.

Justinian, _Institutes_, Lib. II, ch. 1, s. 1.

Chapter 1

INTRODUCTION

The sea has traditionally been relied upon by American society as a means of transportation, a source of food, a place
for enjoyment, and a sink for the disposal of wastes. As a
natural consequence of this reliance, men have congregated
around the natural harbors of the coastal shoreline,[1] where
the colonial settlements founded over three hundred years
ago have since grown into the thickly populated metropolitan
areas of today. Recent census data indicate that fifty-four
percent of the nation's population presently live within the
fifty mile coastal strip[2] that comprises but eight per cent
of the total U.S. land area. Moreover, the distribution of
population has been shifting steadily towards this marine
perimeter[3] as employment opportunities have expanded with
the rapid growth of economic activity in coastal regions.

Although the nature of coastal activity changed as our
industrial economy matured, the land-sea interface has retained its significance as a vital link between American society and the resources that sustain its vitality. Consider, for example, the relationship between the shoreline and
energy-related activities. Petroleum shipments account for
a high percentage of total throughput in many American
ports; electric power plants are increasingly located on the

---

1. Coastal shoreline refers to the land-sea interface of the
contiguous states which border on the Atlantic and Pacific
Oceans, the Gulf of Mexico, and the Great Lakes.

2. This figure excludes Alaska and Hawaii. U.S. Dept. of
Commerce, Bureau of the Census, Statistical Abstract of The
United States - 1972, Table No. 4, at 6.

3. Id.

coast to utilize the waters for cooling purposes; and refinery complexes often cluster about deep-draft harbors
which can accomodate large tankers from abroad.[4]

Throughout its historical period of development, the
coastal shoreline was viewed as relatively limitless in its
capacity to support multiple endeavors. Only in the last
decade has this attitude begun to change, as the nation experiences a growing consensus of dissatisfaction with trends
in the utilization of its environmental resources, especially those in coastal areas where pressures for development are the greatest. Having directed our initial attention to the ecological necessity of water pollution control,
we are coming to realize that the use of land is also a key
ingredient in the management of the coastal environment.
Specifically, we now recognize that important "recreational
amenities" associated with the natural, cultural, scenic,
historic, and aesthetic attributes of coastal areas are
being irretrievably lost to the public in the face of
growing demands for private development.

That the issue of shoreline for the public is a matter of
great concern is best illustrated by the situation with regards the nation's beaches, where the conflict between
public recreation and private use is most acute. In an article written last summer entitled "We Shall Fight Them On
the Beaches...", Anthony Wolff has framed the issues in
eloquent terms:

---

4. All these activities are expected to continue to grow and
will require additional sites along the coastal shoreline in
the near future. This growth of on-shore facilities will also be spurred by increased activity offshore, including mineral and fuel extraction, oil transshipment, and power gen-
eration.

Once again we are in the season of the summer solstice, the high season in the temperate zone, when all mankind heads for the beach. Pale flesh and desiccated spirits yearn to be rebaptised. In this ecumenical rite we are a nation of fundamentalists: nothing less than total immersion in salt water will redeem us.

Inevitably, however, the pilgrimage turns into an ordeal. The mass migration to the beach gets stalled in a summer-long traffic jam that hardens into an unmoving mass of hot metal and boiling frustration on the weekends. There are simply too many people heading for too little beach at the same time.

On holidays, many spend the day oozing along the coast from one public beach to the next in a vain search for a parking place. The lucky ones end up herded together on the sand like seals in a rookery, oiled and broiling in indecent proximity to the whole population they presumably came so far to get away from.

More and more, increasingly leisured and mobile Americans seem to expect access to the beach as something corollary to a constitutional right. But, with 50 percent of us living within fifty miles of a coast, the public beaches are already inadequate to the demand. Even so, the government further incites the public lust for the seashore by building better highways and by tampering with traditional holidays to prolong summer weekends.

In the face of this growing demand—indeed, largely in response to it—the supply of beach open to the public is shrinking even further. Private beach owners and municipalities endowed with town beaches—even those that have always been permissive about peaceable trespass—are in arms against an imminent invasion. At best, they foresee masses of alien refugees from the urban prison. At worst,

they fear vagrant hordes of freeloading,
long-haired barbarians who will smoke pot
and fornicate on the sand without even
paying property taxes.

So everywhere more and more under-popu-
lated beachfront is posted against trespass and patrolled by intolerant gen-
darmes. Landlords extend walls or fences
across their dry-sand beaches to the
waterline. Elaborate security systems restrict municipal beaches to town residents: official windshield stickers are
required at parking lots, while nearby
roadside parking is prohibited. More
liberal towns charge non-residents parking
fees as high as $15 for a single visit.
Pedestrian access to the beach is secured
by plastic-laminated ID cards or numbered
dog tags or bracelets. "Our facilites are
already overcrowded and overutilized,"
complained an official of one Long Island
county last summer. "We have all we can
do to preserve the best facilities for our
own residents."[5]

This annual summer impasse is developing into a confrontation between the
public and the proprietors, who are determined to hold their private beaches for
themselves.

The struggle over sand as described above epitomizes the
problem of decreasing coastal open space for public recreational use, and is typical of the complexity of coastal
resource management issues in general. In potential conflict are the needs for expanded recreational opportunities
for the public (especially in urban areas) on the one hand,
and the desire for intensive private development on the

5. Harper's Magazine, at 55, August, 1973.

other. And both of these activities are constrained by the
existence of powerful natural forces as well as fragile ecological systems.[6] The land-water edge is thus characterized
by an interlocking web of specific individual concerns and
diffuse social and ecological interests. Yet, the economic
and legal regimes regulating man's activities in this zone
were historically intended to protect and serve only the interests of individuals in their dealings with each other,
and have not always been well-suited to maximize the broader
social welfare. Part of this welfare is the opportunity for
the general public to have access to and enjoy the unique
features of the shoreline; but unfortunately, the American
coast has been so exposed to the pressures for private development that only a small percentage is now in public ownership
for recreation.[7] This indicates that traditional institutional arrangements entrusted with the allocation of scarce
coastal resources have been incapable of striking a
socially-optimal balance, not only between conservation and
development, but also between private and public use.

6. See generally Shephard and Wanless, Our Changing Coast-
lines (1971); E. Odum, Fundamentals of Ecology (2d. ed.
1959); R. Parson, Conserving American Resources (2d. ed.
1964).

7. In 1962, a meager six percent of the total U.S. shoreline
judged suitable for recreation was publicly-owned. See Geo.
Washington University, Shoreline Recreation Resources of the
United States, Outdoor Recreation Resources Review Commission Study Report No. 4, at 11 (1962).

The disproportionate amount of shoreline for the public has attracted the attention of the Congress[8] and has influenced the introduction of a variety of legislation designed in whole or in part to deal with the situation.[9] In particular, Congress has enacted into law the Coastal Zone Management Act of 1972,[10] which basically provides matching funds for coastal states to encourage the development and administration of state coastal zone management programs. Among the Congressional findings which prompted this action were as follows:

---

8. See, e.g., Senator Henry Jackson, "Introduction of the National Land Use Policy Act of 1970," Congressional Record - Senate, at 836, January 29, 1970 (open beaches vs. private and commercial development as a dramatic land-use conflict calling for the formulation of a national land-use policy); Senator Ralph Yarborough, "S. 3044 - Introduction of the National Open Beaches Act," Congressional Record-Senate, at 30335, October 16, 1969 ("We are becoming a landlocked people, fenced away from our beautiful shores, unable to exercise the ancient right to enjoy our precious beaches "); Representative Robert Eckhardt, "Eckhardt Open Beaches Legislation," Congressional Record-Extension of Remarks, at 5909, September 19,1973 ("The beaches of the United States are a heritage of all of the people of the Nation. Both the present and future generations of Americans should have the right to enjoyment of this most important natural resource "); See also, Commission on Marine Science, Engineering, and Resources, Our Nation and the Sea, at 70 (1969) (Special attention needed for shoreline recreation problems)

9. The only bill which deals exclusively with the shoreline recreation problem is the proposed National Open Beaches Act, which has been introduced every year by Representative Robert Eckhardt (D-Tex) since 1969. This legislation is discussed infra, Chapter 7, at p.126.

10. Public Law 92-583, 86 Stat. 1280, approved by the 92nd Congress on October 27, 1972. For full text of the Act, see Appendix A, infra, at p. 231.

> The increasing and competing demands
> upon the lands and waters of our coastal
> zone occasioned by population growth and
> economic development...have resulted in
> the loss of living marine resources,
> wildlife,nutrient-rich areas, permanent and
> adverse changes to ecological systems,
> decreasing open space for public use, and
> shoreline erosion;
>
> ...Important ecological, cultural, histo-
> ric, and aesthetic values in the coastal
> zone which are essential to the well-being
> of all citizens are being irretrievably
> damaged or lost;
>
> ...Special natural and scenic characteris-
> tics are being damaged by ill-planned de-
> velopment that threatens these val-
> ues;...11 (Emphasis added).

Having articulated a national concern for what we have termed "recreational amenities" in coastal areas, the Congress went on to declare it the national policy:

> (a) to preserve, protect, develop, and
> where possible, to restore or enhance, the
> resources of the Nation's coastal zone for
> this and succeeding generations, (and)
>
> (b) to encourage and assist the states to
> exercise effectively their responsibil-
> ities in the coastal zone through the de-
> velopment and implementation of management
> programs to achieve wise use of the land
> and water resources of the coastal zone
> giving full consideration to ecological,
> cultural, historic, and aesthetic values
> as well as to needs for economic develop-
> ment,...12 (Emphasis added).

---

11. Id., at secs. 302 (c), (e), (f).

12. Id., at secs. 303 (a), (b). See also sec. 306 (c) (9), which requires state management programs to establish 'proce-dures whereby specific areas may be designated for the pur-pose of preserving or restoring them for their conservation, recreational, ecological, or esthetic values."

This language clearly indicates that an important part of
the intent of Congress in enacting this legislation was to
enhance the opportunities for the general public to share in
the unique experiences available at the land-sea interface.
This intent is also reflected in the legislative history of
the act, where recreation (including beaches, parks, wildlife, preserves, sports fishing, swimming, and pleasure
boating) and related open space uses (including educational
and natural preserves, scenic beauty, and public access to
the coastline and coastal and estuarine areas, both physical
and visual) were suggested as elements that should be included in state management programs.[13] Finally, the administrative construction of the Act by the federal agency
charged with its implementation seems to indicate that the
public access question will be one of the things the federal
approval team will look for in reviewing state coastal zone
management programs.[14]

Of the 34 coastal state and territories that are eligible
for program development grants under the Coastal Zone
Management Act of 1972, approximately 29 have indicated an
intent to apply for funding. This report is intended to
serve as an input to the processes of policy-making and

13. Senate Committee on Commerce, Report on S. 3507 - National Coastal Zone Management Act of 1972, Report No.
92-753, at 11 (1972).

14. This inference is based on testimony by Robert Knecht,
Director of the Office of Coastal Environment, National
Oceanic and Atmospheric Administration, U. S. Department of
Commerce, appearing before the House Merchant Marine Subcom-
mittee on Fisheries and Wildlife, October 25-26, 1973. See
Coastal Zone Management Newsletter at 6, Nautilus Press,
Inc., Washington, D.C. (October 31, 1973).

planning which these states will then have to undertake in
connection with public recreational use of their coastal
shorelines. In the process, we shall explore fully the economic, political, and legal regimes surrounding the allocation and use of the shoreline for private and public
purposes;[15] and we shall examine the tools that are
available for the implementation of public policy in this
regard. It must be pointed out, however, that this is but
an initial cut at the problem, intended only to lay the
groundwork for the formulation of public policy guidelines.
Isolating a problem and evaluating the techniques available
to carry out its solution are necessary but not sufficient
components in the process of making equitable and efficient
choices among policy alternatives. In the concluding
chapter of this report, a number of critical decision-making
issues will be outlined and left for resolution to the results of experience and future study, and the evolution of
social values.

Before proceeding into the body of this report, a word
about philosophy of approach is in order. While solid arguments can be made in favor of expanding public recreational
opportunities in the nation's shoreline, we must always bear
in mind that advances in this particular sector of the public welfare will never be without costs to other sectors.

---

15. The analysis of the social and economic dimensions of
the shoreline recreational problem (Part One) is based in
part on previous work by the author, including: Power, Pollution, and Public Policy, MIT Press, at Chapters 1 and 3
(1972); "The Crisis in Shoreline Recreation Lands", Papers
on National Land Use Policy Issues, U.S. Senate Committee on
Interior and Insular Affairs (1971); and "Understanding the
Allocative System: A Framework for the Management of
Coastal Resources," presented at 8th Annual Conference of
the Marine Technology Society (1972).

More public recreation in coastal areas may threaten certain conservation objectives or come at the expense of established private interests. In assessing these tradeoffs, we must remember two things. First, while man is a social being performing social activities like recreation, he is also a biological organism whose survival as a species depends on the maintenance of an intricately complex, ecological balance among himself and all other plant and animal species within their respective geological and climatic environments.[16] The many forms of fish and wildlife found solely in the coastal and estuarine zones are an integral part of this ecosystem, together with all other life-forms that exist in the beach, bluff, and wetland areas of the shoreline. There is a clear and pressing need to preserve the vitality of all such ecological systems, at the very least until man can determine their ultimate importance as a component part of his own life cycle and those of other forms of life on this planet. To the extent that recreation or any other human activity threatens to significantly disrupt these natural systems, man must be willing to yield in their favor.

The second thing that we must remember in dealing with the issue of shoreline for the public is that existing property rights are built on expectations that have not enjoyed the long-standing protection of the law without good

---

16. See Webber, et al., Trends in American Living and Outdoor Recreation, U.S. Outdoor Recreation Resources Review Commission Study Report No. 22, at 248, Washington, D.C. (1962).

reason.[17] This is the doctrine that an ounce of history is worth a pound of logic, and it has succinctly been applied to recreation planning by a leading writer in the field, who has observed:

> ... any attempted solution to the problem of satisfying public recreational needs which fails to recognize the present pattern of private rights, or the need to effect change in an orderly and planned manner, must fail.[18]

Hopefully, adherence to this concept, coupled with a recognition that untrammelled public use is the surest way to despoil a fragile ecological resource, will help keep the analysis contained herein as balanced and productive as possible.

---

17. As the legal scholar Blackstone noted:

> There is nothing which so generally strikes the imagination, and engages the affections of mankind, as the right of property, or that sole and despotic dominion which one man claims and exercises over the external things of the world, in total exclusion of any other individual in the universe.

1 Cooley's Blackstone 321 (Book II, Ch. 1 of W. Blackstone, Commentaries on the Law of England). While this notion of property rights may be somewhat outdated in the strictly legal sense, it serves to illustrate the fervor with which some individuals view their command over the resources of the earth.

18. Reis, "Policy and Planning for Recreational Use of Inland Water," 40 Temple L.Q. 155, at 180 (1967).

Part I

THE SOCIAL AND ECONOMIC DIMENSIONS OF THE
SHORELINE RECREATION PROBLEM

Chapter 2

THE NEED AND THE DEMAND FOR SHORELINE RECREATION OPPORTUNITIES

1. The Need for Outdoor Recreation

Since the earliest days of planning for outdoor recreation, great emphasis has been laid on the value of outdoor recreation in helping "cure" the ills of society. Many advocates of outdoor recreation described parks, playgrounds, beaches, and other opportunities for recreational activity as "veritable cure-alls which would isolate young people from and immunize them against the delinquency, alcoholism, prostitution, and crime that abounded in slums."[1] In later years, the emphasis shifted to the value of outdoor recreation in counteracting the harmful effects of the stress and tensions of life in an urban-industrial society. Recreation generally came to be viewed as a major solution to the problems of mental illness that were attributed to such tensions.

Herbert Gans, the noted sociologist, has taken issue with this orientation towards a causal link between recreation and mental health:

> . . . (These attitudes were) developed by a culturally narrow reform group which was reacting to a deplorable physical and social environment and rejected the coming of the urban-industrial society. As a result, it glorified the simple rural life and hoped to use outdoor recreation as a means of maintaining at least some vestige

1. Gans, <u>People and Plans</u>, Basic Books, Inc., New York, N.Y. (1968), at 109.

of a traditional society and culture.
Given these conditions and motivations, no
one saw fit to investigate the relationship between outdoor recreation and mental
health empirically.[2]

How then can we go about determining what relationship,
if any, exists between recreation and mental health, or, in
broader terms, the general health and well-being of man in
modern society? Most psychologists and sociologists would
concur that the human predicament can best be described as
the task of maintaining a balance, both internally and ex-
ternally, between man's existence as an _organism_ and as a
personality. This predicament has been described by
Lawrence K. Frank:

So long as man lives, he must function as
an organism through his **continual** inter-
course with the natural environment,
breathing, eating, eliminating, sleeping,
and sexual functioning as a mammalian
organism. Thus, as an organism, man is
continually exposed to a variety of biological and psychological signals to which
he is more or less susceptible; but, as a
personality, he must strive to live in his
symbolic cultural world, exhibiting the
orderly patterned conduct and required
performance in response to the symbols and
rituals of his social order. He
finds himself often "tempted" by these po-
tent biological signals but continually
reminded by the symbols and especially by
the expectations of other persons, of the
group-sanctioned code of conduct he is
expected to observe. This conflict is
lifelong and apparently inescapable unless
the individual withdraws completely from

2. Id.

> social life in some form of mental dis-
> orders. A crucial problem for mental
> health is how an individual can resolve
> this conflict without incurring high costs
> psychologically and persistent damage to
> his personality, and what sources he can
> rely upon for strength and renewal in fac-
> ing his life tasks.[3] (Emphasis added)

In this spirit, Herbert Gans has described mental health as "the ability of an individual as an occupier of social roles and as a personality to move toward the achievement of his vision of the good life and the good society . . . mental health is a social rather than an individual concept, because if society frustrates the movement toward the good life, the mental health of those involved may be affected."[4] There are considerable present day indications that society does tend in many ways to frustrate an individual's movement toward the good life, and that it is increasingly difficult to maintain the balance necessary for well-being as described above. The characteristics and intensity of the emotional stresses and strains of modern life have been stated (and sometimes overstated) by many writers. There can be no doubt that the pollution, congestion, noise, and other social ills of the urban environment detract from the well-being of those who live and work in metropolitan areas. These "sensory overloads" have particularly severe effects on the low-income, less mobile groups

---

3. Frank, et al., Trends in American Living and Outdoor Recreation, U.S. Outdoor Recreation Resources Review Commission (ORRRC) Study Report No. 22 (1962), at 249.

4. See Gans, op. cit. note 1 supra, at 112.

that now dominate the central cities, where the overload is compounded by extreme crowding and oppressive living conditions, by widespread nutritional inadequacies, and by the frustrations of unemployment, drug addiction, and high crime rates.

Having established that health can best be understood as a product of the interaction between an individual and the total physical and social environment that he experiences, and recognizing some of the impedients to the maintenance of a healthly sociological balance in this interaction with present-day society, we must now ask: What part can outdoor recreation play in helping the individual maintain this balance so vital to his mental health and physical well-being? Once again, it is Gans who provides us with the most incisive approach:

> . . . the recognition of the limited significance of outdoor recreation in the treatment of personality disorders should not blind us to the potential significance of it for developing and sustaining healthly personalities. Indeed, we may find that recreation, especially outdoor recreation, provides one of the most promising approaches to the elusive goal of mental health as a form of "primary prevention" of mental ill health. In and through outdoor recreation the individual, especially in early life, may develop the self-confidence, the elasticity, and spontaneity for action and expression of feelings which will enable him to cope with city living and indoor working, while maintaining his physical and mental health.[5] (Emphasis added)

---

5. Id.

So while the arguments for the psychological and emotional need for outdoor activity may have been overstated,[6] it seems clear that outdoor recreation can be a renewing experience, a refreshing change from the working routine. But the view each individual takes of outdoor recreation depends on his preferences and personality, is conditioned by his physical and economic environment, and is influenced by his age and sex. From this we can see that the collection of more extensive data on leisure behavior is immensely important, since the formation of long-term outdoor recreation policy presents a wide variety of sociological issues not easy to define or resolve. Lawrence Frank has suggested[7] that we can better plan for recreation if we can discover what needs and aspirations people are trying to fulfill and if we can recognize what may be blocking or frustrating their quest. But in the absence of empirical evidence on these questions, what should be our approach to planning? The fact that the demand for outdoor recreational activity is strong and increasing rapidly suggests that we should adopt a user-oriented approach. As one commentator has pointed out:

---

6.   ". . . it is by no means clear that everyone or even a majority of persons, suffers from severe strains and stresses; moreover, a substantial proportion of the population apparently rarely or never engages in outdoor recreation. . . Although much is made of the increase in tension and strain, yet it is a fact that no comprehensive continuous effort has ever been made to measure these factors."

Clawson and Kretch, The Economics of Outdoor Recreation, John Hopkins Press, Baltimore, Md. (1966), at 31.

7. See Frank, op cit. note 3 supra, at 220.

> . . . to ask whether outdoor recreation is
> important to the mental health of
> Americans is, in one sense, tantamount to
> asking whether the full and rich life is
> important; and the answer of course is
> clear . . . the degree of crowding at our
> parks, our ski slopes, beaches, picnic
> sites, and even our mountain trails is
> clear evidence of the popular response to
> this question.[8]

What then, is the demand for outdoor recreational opportunities, and which facilities are used and preferred by
those who seek this satisfying leisure-time activity?

2. The Demand for Outdoor Recreation

Recreation has always been a prime objective of American
life; indeed, the "pursuit of happiness" is firmly established in the Declaration of Independence as a basic human right. It has been noted that most Americans, when
given the opportunity to diminish their "sensory overload"
through a change of routine, "will spend a summer afternoon
in a suburban backyard around a barbecue, in a city park,
or at the nearest swimming pool or beach. Given the chance
and the means for a vacation away from home, they will take
to the country, the mountains, or the seashore."[9] It is
not surprising, then, that the demand for outdoor recreation is surging, spurred on by increases in the causal
factors of population, disposable income, leisure, mo-

8. Webber, et al., Trends in American Living and Outdoor
Recreation, U.S. Outdoor Recreation Resources Review Commission, Study Report No. 22 (1962), at 249.

9. Id.

bility, education, and overall standard of living. The
Outdoor Recreation Resources Review Commission (ORRRC), in
a report to Congress in 1962 entitled Outdoor Recreation
for America,[10] noted and documented these causal factors
and their influence on recreational demands. It was the
conclusion of this report that, as the levels of these
factors rose, the growth of outdoor recreation demand would
accelerate even faster, and in a sustained fashion, then
the net increase in population:

> Whatever the measuring rod . . . it is
> clear that Americans are seeking the out-
> doors as never before. And this is only a
> foretaste of what is to come. Not only
> will there be many more people, they will
> want to do more and they will have more
> money and time to do it with. By 2000 the
> population should double; the demand for
> recreation should triple.[11]

By 1965, it was clear that these projections significantly
underestimated the mushrooming demand. A survey conducted
by the Bureau of Outdoor Recreation found that increases in
major summertime outdoor recreation activities over the
period 1960-1965 had "far surpassed" the earlier predictions; and revised projections indicated that participation in these activities would be quadruple the 1960
level by the year 2000.[12] These trends translate into a ten

---

10. U.S. Department of the Interior, Bureau of Outdoor Re-
creation, Outdoor Recreation for America, A Report to the
President and Congress by the Outdoor Recreation Resources
Review Commission (1962).

11. Id.

12. U.S. Bureau of Outdoor Recreation, 1965 Survey of Outdoor Recreation Activities, Washington, D.C. (1967).

to twelve per cent annual increase in the use of public recreation areas.[13]

In addition to outlining the general trends in outdoor recreation activity, the 1960 survey documented the patterns in demand as expressed by participation rates and user days. These indicators are listed in Table 1 for various outdoor activities. An examination of these and other related data[14] reveal a number of interesting trends. The first major trend of note is that Americans most frequently participate in simple activities that are usually independent of age, income, education, or occupation. Driving and walking for pleasure, playing outdoor games, swimming, and sightseeing lead the list of outdoor pursuits in annual days of activity per person, with driving and walking together accounting for almost forty-three per cent of these days. A second trend of importance is the great demand for activity close to home. People seeking outdoor recreation do so within definite time periods that can be classified as day outings, weekend or overnight trips, and vacations. The most frequent of these is the day outing, which is presently considered the fundamental unit of outdoor recreation. Most indications are that people will drive one way about two hours -- a distance that may vary from 30 miles to as much as 90 miles -- for such out-

---

13. Over the period 1920-1964, national park attendance rose from one million to one hundred million. From 1942-1964, state park attendance increased from sixty-nine million to two hundred eighty-five million. Clawson, op. cit. note 6 supra, at 5.

14. See U.S. Outdoor Recreation Resources Review Commission, National Recreation Survey, Study Report No. 19, Washington, D.C. (1962).

Table 1. Patterns of Demand for Selected Outdoor Recreation
Activities in the U.S.--1960*

Activity and Per Cent Participating (Summer '60)	Days per Participant (Summer '60)	Days per Person (Summer '60)	Days per Person (Annual '60)
Physically Active Recreation:			
Playing Outdoor Games & Sports (30)	12.3	3.63	12.71
Bicycling (9)	19.4	1.75	5.17
Horseback Riding (6)	7.5	.42	1.25
Water Sports:			
Swimming (45)	11.5	5.15	6.47
Canoeing (2)	3.0	.07	.12
Sailing (2)	3.0	.05	.11
Other Boating (22)	5.5	1.22	1.95
Water Skiing (6)	5.1	.30	.41
Fishing (29)	6.8	1.99	4.19
Backwoods Recreation:			
Camping (8)	5.7	.46	.86
Hiking (6)	4.4	.26	.42
Mountain Climbing (1)	3.7	.04	.09
Hunting (3)	5.6	.19	1.86
Passive Outdoor Pursuits:			
Picnicking (53)	4.0	2.14	3.53
Walking for Pleasure (33)	13.1	4.34	17.93
Driving for Pleasure (52)	12.7	6.68	20.73
Sightseeing (42)	5.2	2.20	5.91
Attending Outdoor Sports Events (24)	5.5	1.32	3.75
Nature Walks (14)	5.2	.75	2.07
Attending Outdoor Concerts (9)	2.4	.21	.39
Miscellaneous (5)	8.4	.40	.57

*Rates shown are for persons twelve years and over

Source: U.S. Outdoor Recreation Resources Review Commission, National Recreation Survey, Study Report No. 19, Washington, D.C. (1962).

standing recreation sites as ocean beaches or scenic camp-
grounds. For the weekend or overnight outing, the median
travel distance is about 90 to 125 miles. While some vaca-
tioners will travel many miles on week or two-week-long
vacations, by far the greatest demands are placed on the
facilities serving daily and weekend outings. Hence,
pressures are greatest within about 125 miles of metropolitan centers, with maximum demands at those facilities in
close proximity to the central cities. This has lead one
commentator to observe:

> . . .[today's problems] do not center on
> the acquisition of unique and dramatic re-
> sources for the public, but on the broad
> availability of outdoor recreation for ev-
> eryone and often; nearby open areas for
> weekend visits by moderate-income urba-
> nites are more characteristic of our re-
> creation needs than the trip to a far away
> area of unforgettable beauty by the fort-
> unate persons who can get there.[15]

The importance of providing outdoor recreation facilities
close to where people live is highlighted by the fact that,
in the inner cities, one finds the lowest rates of participation associated with low-income and poorly-educated
people living in oppressive surroundings. Outdoor recreation does not play an important role in the leisure time of
these groups due to the lack of nearby facilities and the
lack of money and adequate transportation to get to more

---

15. Perloff and Wingo, Trends in American Living and Outdoor Recreation, U.S. Outdoor Recreation Resources Review
Commission Study Report No. 22, Washington, D.C. (1962),
at 82.

distant areas. But while outdoor opportunities are most
urgently needed close to metropolitan areas, the scarcity
of land and intense competition for private development
often result in low per capita provision of urban recreation facilities.[16]

The final major trend to be noted is the pervasive at-
traction for water-oriented activities, as described in the
final report of the ORRRC:

> Most people seeking outdoor recreation
> want water to sit by, to swim and fish in,
> to ski across, to dive under and to run
> their boats over. Swimming is now one of
> the most popular outdoor activities and is
> likely to be the most popular of all by
> the turn of the century. Boating and
> fishing are among the top 10 activities.
> Camping, picnicking, and hiking, also high
> on the list, are more attractive near
> water sites.[17]

Of the outdoor activities listed in Table 1, water sports
accounted for 14.6 per cent of the annual user days per
person and 26 percent of the summertime user days, while 44
per cent of outdoor recreation participants favored
water-based activities over any others. Among water
sports, swimming is the most prominent. It has by far the
largest participation rate; is more highly associated with
other activities;[18] seems to have special importance to ur-

---

16. For a general discussion of problems and approaches to
the urban recreation issue, see National League of Cities,
Recreation in the Nation's Cities, prepared for the U.S.
Bureau of Outdoor Recreation, Washington, D.C. (1968).

17. U.S. Dept. of the Interior, op. cit. note 10 supra, at
4.

18. See U.S. Outdoor Recreation Resources Review Commission, op. cit. note 14 supra, at 6.

ban dwellers, whose participation rate is 49 per cent versus 38 per cent for the non-urban population; and is even preferred by 17 per cent of those not participating in outdoor recreation. This preference for swimming was confirmed by the 1965 Bureau of Outdoor Recreation survey, which reported that swimming had attained second place in user participation and was becoming so popular that it will be our number one outdoor recreation activity by 1980.[19] The survey found that, in 1965, 48 per cent of the population (12 years and over) swam an average of 14.3 days each; 30 per cent went fishing an average of 7.6 days; 24 per cent went boating an average of 6.5 times; and 6 per cent went water skiing an average of 6.6 times.[20] More recently, the preliminary results of a 1970 Bureau of Outdoor Recreation survey indicate that per capita participation in both swimming and boating activities has risen nearly 50 per cent from 1960 levels, from 6.47 to 9 days per person annually.[21]

3. The Social and Economic Significance of Shoreline Recreation

This outline of the proportions of future demand for outdoor recreation holds clear implications with regards the

---

19. U.S. Bureau of Outdoor Recreation, op. cit. note 12 supra.

20. Id., at 9-11.

21. U.S. Bureau of Outdoor Recreation, The 1970 Survey of Outdoor Recreation Activities: Preliminary Report, Washington, D.C. (1972), at 9.

future of shoreline recreation. Recreation is already one
of the largest and fastest-growing uses of the coastal
zone,[22] and will increase in importance with continuing increases in coastal population, leisure time, income, and mobility. Coastal cities are generally the focal points of
coastal tourism and recreation, serving not only to produce
recreationists but also to attract them. The future level
of shoreline recreational activities is indicated by Table
2, which lists projected growth rates for selected

Table 2. Projected Growth in Shoreline Recreational Activities

Activity	Annual Growth Rate* (per cent)	Coastal Participation 1975** (millions)
Swimming	3.8	40
Boating	4.0	14
Fishing	1.8	16
Surfing	3.0	4
Skin Diving	5.0	3

*Sources:

Swimming, boating, fishing--U. S. Bureau of Outdoor Recreation, 1965 Survey of Outdoor Recreation Activities (1967);

surfing--Merrill, Lynch, Pierce, Fenner and Smith, Inc.,
Leisure-Investment Opportunities in a $150 Billion Market
(1968), at 7;

skindiving--Winslow & Bigler, "A New Perspective on Recreational Use of the Ocean", Undersea Technology, vol. 10,
no. 7 (July, 1969), at 52.

**Source: University of Rhode Island, New England Marine
Resources Information Program, Outdoor Recreational Uses of
Coastal Areas, No. 1 (1969), at 18.

22. See Ketchum, ed., The Water's Edge - Critical Problems
of the Coastal Zone, M.I.T. Press (1972), at 84 et seq.

water-oriented recreation activities together with antici-
pated levels of participation in these activities in the
coastal zone by 1975. These figures are staggering when we
consider that the supply of public recreational facilities
is essentially fixed, and most of these facilities are
already filled to capacity. Consider, for example, this
excerpt from a Massachusetts report on public outdoor recreation:

> . . . 80 percent of the ocean beach capa-
> city lies within the Metropolitan Parks
> District, where 2 million people, more
> than 40 per cent of the State's popula-
> tion, live. Within this district, where
> the beaches can accomodate 15 per cent of
> the resident population, use on peak days
> taxes their capacity heavily. [23]

Interestingly enough, this was the situation is <u>1954</u>. By
1970, this population had risen to approximately 2.8 million, or 48 per cent of the state total,[24] without a cor-
respondingly large increase in public beach facilities.
Anyone who has been delayed for hours on a hot day in
bumper-to-bumper traffic to the Cape Cod shore, or who has
experienced the mobs of people at the Revere and Lynn
beaches north of Boston, can attest to the severity of this
situation. A similar shortage exists with boating facilities in some areas, where there are so many boats at anchor
that room for turn-arounds is fast disappearing. In Rhode
Island, for example, over three hundred new pleasure boats

---

23. Commonwealth of Massachusetts, Department of Natural
Resources, <u>Public Outdoor Recreation</u> (1954).

24. See U.S. Dept. of Commerce, <u>Statistical Abstract of
the United States - 1972</u>, Washington, D.C. (1972), at 838.

are bought annually, each of which will require accomo-
dations for mooring and servicing. These observations
regarding the disproportionate situation between shoreline
demand and supply will be further discussed in Chapter
Three.

The fact that hordes of recreationists crowd the beaches
and other coastal recreational facilities, especially near
the cities, points to the intrinsic value of the shoreline
as a public resource. This social importance has been
noted by the ORRRC:

> Of the many outdoor recreation "environ-
> ments" -- mountains, seacoasts, deserts,
> and woodlands -- the shoreline seems to
> have an unusually strong appeal for Amer-
> icans.[25]

Why this propensity for water-related activity, especially
at the coastal shores? Some possible explanations offered
by one commentator are as follows:

> Perhaps it is an adaption of our frontier
> traditions to the conditions of modern
> life. It may be a reflection of a
> deep-seated desire for some activity in
> which the whole family can join. To some
> extent, it may a flight from urban living,
> or even from the new suburbs, to a more
> direct contact with nature. Water-
> centered recreation is often associated
> with less congestion and regimentation.
> Perhaps the tactile sensations -- direct
> immersion in air, water, and sunshine with

---

25. George Washington University, Shoreline Recreation Resources of the United States, U.S. Outdoor Recreation Resources Review Commission Study Report No. 4, Washington,
D.C. (1962), at 10.

less screening from clothing -- explain
its appeal to many.[26]

While such sociological and psychological considerations may be fairly debatable as causal factors, the wide variety of easy, active forms of recreational activity that the shoreline supports cannot be denied as a motivational force. The neritic or near-shore zone extending from the continental shelf to the beach is well-suited for motor boating, sailing, waterskiing, skindiving, and fishing. Beaches, in most cases, offer the cheapest and most enjoyable recreation uses for large numbers of people:

> Going into the surf is fun whether one swims or not. It is not necessary to be a mountain climber to take walks along the beach, and beachcombing is an activity that appeals to everyone from toddler to octogenerian . . . here, land and water are easily accessible; the violence of breaking surf and the warm safety of relaxing sands are but a step apart; the stimulation of the foreign environment of the water and the relaxation of sunbathing are nowhere else so easy of choice. Physical sport and mental relaxation are equally available.[27]

---

26. Moore, "The Rise of Reservoir Recreation," Economic Studies of Outdoor Recreation, ORRRC Study Report No. 24, Wash. D. C. (1962), at 24; See also Ditton, The Social and Economic Significance of Recreation Activities in the Marine Environment, Univ. of Michigan Sea Grant Program, Technical Report No. 11 (1972).

27. See George Washington University, op. cit. note 25 supra, at 4.

Shoreland areas adjacent to beaches support many other
activities, such as sightseeing, picnicing, camping, and
walking. An additional use of coastal areas, and probably
the most widespread, is for aesthetic enjoyment, including
nature watching in a salt marsh, painting, or sightseeing
along a bluff shoreline:

> Viewing the deep and unbroken vistas over
> the sea, watching for ocean-going vessels,
> feeling the brisk flow of the sea-breeze,
> contemplating the historic past and
> legends of the sea, and possibly seeing
> porpoises or whales on the horizon are
> just a few of the special activities that
> are extremely meaningful to visitors at
> the seacoast.[28]

In short, almost all forms of outdoor recreation activity
are greatly enhanced by proximity to the ocean, whose
unique mix of resource attributes contributes to a strong
leisure appeal. And, as one commentator has noted
recently, "a variety of resources in addition to the
sea--such as bays, estuaries, river mouths and deltas, and
mountain scenery backdrops--all add materially to the
physical and psychological appeal for recreational uses.
The compounding of many resource features in close juxta-
position adds materially to the strength of attributes
taken separately."[29]

All of the above values associated with shoreline resources are of course magnified by their physical accessibility to large populations, and can be measured to some
extent in economic terms. Recreation is America's fourth

---

28. Ketchum, ed., op. cit. note 22 supra, at 91.
29. Id.

largest and fastest growing industry, and economists
estimate that the total leisure industry market could reach
$250 billion by 1975, with total <u>outdoor</u> recreation
expenditures expected to reach $83 billion.[30] With respect
to shoreline recreation, it has been estimated that in 1968
approximately 112 million people participated in a total of
7.1 billion ocean-oriented occasions and spent about $14
billion.[31] Roughly 20 million people now engage in boating
in the coastal zone, with the number of boats increasing at
the rate of 200,000 per year.[32] In 1965, it is estimated
that over 8 million salt water anglers spent $800 million
on this sport alone.[33] By 1975, the total ocean-recreation
market is forecast to reach $23.5 billion, or 28 per cent
of total outdoor recreation expenditures.[34] The recreational boating market is expected to account for $1 billion
of this coastal business, while swimming, surfing, skindiving, and sport fishing are expected to generate another
$4.4 billion in revenues.[35] While additional economic data

---

30. Jensen, <u>Outdoor Recreation in America</u>, Burgess Publishing Co. (1970), at 214.

31. Winslow & Bigler, "A New Perspective on Recreational
Use of the Ocean", <u>Undersea Technology</u>, vol. 10, no. 7
(July, 1969), at 51.

32. See National Council on Marine Resources and Engineering Development, <u>Marine Science Affairs--A Year of Broadened Participation</u>, Washington, D.C. (1970).

33. U.S. Bureau of Sport Fisheries and Wildlife, "National
Survey of Fishing and Hunting", Resource Publication No.
27, Washington, D.C. (1965).

34. Winslow & Bigler, op. cit. note 31 <u>supra</u>, at 53.

35. University of Rhode Island, New England Marine Resources Information Program, <u>Outdoor Recreation Uses of</u>
<u>Coastal Areas</u>, No. 7 (1969), at 13.

with regards shoreline recreation is conspicuously lacking for specific marine regions, it is abundantly clear that coastal tourism and recreation are significant and growing generators of economic activity throughout the nation.

4. Factors Constraining Recreational Use of Shoreline Resources

While water-based recreation activity is projected to increase dramatically in the future, we must be cognizant of the fact that growth predictions are based on historical participation rates which cannot be extropolated independently of a number of limiting factors. The two major categories of limitations are: (1) the suitability of particular areas for recreational purposes; and (2) the availability of suitable areas to potential users.

The suitability of coastal areas for recreation depends on the type of shoreline involved, its environmental carrying capacity, and the quality of the adjacent water. There are three basic shoreline units[36]--beach, bluff, and wetland-- and, of these, sand beaches can support the widest variety of recreational use. Bluff shores, characterized by banks or cliffs immediately landward of a narrow beach, provide safe harbor areas for recreational boating or unique scenic vistas and rugged isolation for hikers, campers, sightseers, and nature watchers. Wetlands, characterized by tidal or non-tidal marsh, are in lesser demand as public recreational areas but are most valuable in the ecological sense due to the wide range of marine biological

---

36. See George Washington University, op. cit. note 25 supra, at 10-12.

organisms they support.[37]

When compared to most other human activities that utilize coastal resources, it is clear that recreation in general ranks relatively low in terms of environmental impact.

> Whenever a visitor views the panorama, whenever he uses a boat on the water, whenever he runs along the beach, and whenever he studies the historic lore and background of a coastal city, he leaves the resource virtually the same as he found it as far as his principal recreational activity is concerned. . . . The product of tourism and recreation is the individual experience. As such, it is composed not so much of material goods as of psychological impact. Therefore, what one experienced today may be replicated day after day by thousands more with virtually no decay in the resource.[38]

This, of course, is not meant to minimize the danger of adverse effects associated with constructed facilities which often accompany the recreational experience. Beaches, for example, are susceptible to the destructive forces of erosion, often spurred by irresponsible development right at the water's edge. Sand dunes, which act as natural barriers to wind, wave, and current forces, can be destroyed by widespread trampling of their supporting vegetation.[39] Bluff shores, though not particularly vulnerable to the action of currents, are erodable under wave attack and can be weakened by improper shore construction. Finally,

---

37. See generally Niering, The Life of the Marsh McGraw-Hill, (1967).

38. Ketchum, ed., op. cit. note 22 supra, at 93.

39. See McHarg, Design With Nature (Doubleday, 1967), at 7.

wetland areas are extremely susceptible to damage caused by
pollution or dredging and filling for residential or com-
merical use.

Aside from shoreline type and sensitivity to use, water
quality exerts an important influence on the suitability of
a given shoreline area (particularly beaches) for recreational purposes:

> The quality of water is as important as
> the amount of surface acres, miles of
> banks, or location. Polluted water in the
> ocean, a lake, a river, or a reservoir is
> of little use for recreation. Pollution
> by human or industrial waste is only one
> aspect of quality which conditions the
> available supply. The silt load, the
> bottom condition, temperature, and aquatic
> plants also effect the usability of water
> for recreation.[40]

The second major factor that serves to constrain public
recreational use of the shoreline is the availability of
suitable areas, in both the legal and the physical sense.
In the case of beaches, for example, private ownership and
municipal control of parking facilities for local residents
only are forms of legal restrictions on public use of these
shore areas.   In general, then, the only beaches widely
available to the public are public beaches, and even some

---

40. Dept. of the Interior, op. cit. note 10 supra, at 70;
See also Ditton, Water Based Recreation: Access, Water
Quality, and Incompatible Use Considerations - An Interdis-
ciplinary Bibliography, Council of Planning Librarians, Ex-
change Bibliography No. 193 (1970), at 5. Investigation of
public perception of water quality has shown that the presence of algae is the most important indicator of pollution
to most people, with murky water ranking second.   See
David, "Public Perceptions of Water Quality", Water Resources Research, vol. 7, no. 3 (1971), at 453.

of these are restricted.[41] And where public beaches are few and far between, the physical dimension of availability comes into play. One aspect of this is the discouraging effect of crowding both on the beaches and on the highways which lead to them. The other aspect concerns accessibility as a function of each user's income and mobility. While certain middle-to-upper income groups can afford either second homes or extended stays at distant vacation areas, the majority of people prefer recreation within about 90 miles of home, and low-income groups are generally confined to the immediate vicinity of the metropolitan areas. In both places, suitable public facilities may be in short supply due to intense competition with commercial, shipping, and industrial interests (in the urban areas) or with private residential development (in the exurban areas).

5. Concluding Remarks

The demand for outdoor recreation, especially that which is water-oriented, is growing rapidly as the trends toward more leisure time, more real income, and greater mobility enable larger proportions of our growing population to seek recreation activity of all types. The American coastal shoreline, as a unique recreational resource, is ideally situated to accomodate a wide range of these activities; most planners agree that the "hidden demands" for recreational use of this resource are enormous, limited only by the effective supply. The question we must now ask is: To

41. George Washington University, op. cit. note 25 supra, at 5.

what extent has the public interest in the shoreline as a recreational asset been represented in the allocation of coastal lands among competing users? This is the topic for discussion in the remaining chapters of Part One.

Chapter 3

THE SUPPLY OF SHORELINE RECREATION RESOURCES

1. Introduction

Every coastal region of the United States has both natural and cultural resources that are ideal for use in tourism, active and passive recreation, and aesthetic enjoyment. Examples include the glaciated coasts of New England and the Pacific Northwest; the straight barrier beaches and long estuaries from New York to Chesapeake Bay; the cuspate foreland and straight barrier coasts from Cape Hatteras to the Florida Keys; the beaches, swamps, deltas, and barrier islands of the Gulf Coast; the island-sheltered beaches and rugged bluffs of California; and the lowland coasts of Alaska and the volcanic coasts of Hawaii. These shores are endowed with a wealth of water life, vegetation cover, interesting topography, supportive climate, and historical and visual/cultural characteristics. Yet, as a nation, we presently face a shortage of shoreline recreational opportunities for the public. The mushrooming demand for the unique recreational experience that the coastal environment provides has far outstripped the effective supply of suitable resources, particularly near urban areas where the needs are greatest. The situation has aptly been described by Bayard Webster, of the New York Times:

> The shoreline of the United States has been so built up, industrialized and polluted during the last decade that there are relatively few beaches left for the family in search of a free, solitary hour by the sea.
>
> From Maine to Florida and on around to Texas, from Southern California up to

Washington State, the nation's seashores
have become cluttered with hotels, motels,
sprawling developments, military complexes
and industries of every kind.

Miles of tranquil beaches where hun-
dreds of seaside retreats were once open
to everyone for swimming or fishing have
been fouled by oil spills, industrial
effluents, farm pesticides and city sewage.

What remains - shoreland that is not
dirty, crowded or closed to the public -
amounts to a tiny fraction of the
country's total coastal zone, about 1,200
miles or 5 percent of the shore areas
considered suitable for recreation or
human habitation.

The prospect of continuing encroachment, together with the intensified natural erosion often caused by heedless
development (even in normal weather, winds
and waves can eat away or shift up to 20
feet of beach a year), has alarmed many
marine biologists and conservationists.

Close to the heart of the problem are
two factors . . . One is the sharp increase in recent years in the nation's
population. The other is the rush to the
large coastal cities by millions of people
from inland rural areas.

The result is that popular demand for
open recreational space near the water is
rising just as private and industrial
developers are fencing off the best of
it - if not the last of it in any given
area - and land prices are spiraling far
beyond the means of most urban dwellers.[1]

---

1. Webster, "Few Seaside Beaches Left Open in Developers'
Rush," New York Times, March 29, 1970, at 54.

Mr. Webster has touched on all pertinent issues relative to the supply of shoreline recreational resources, and we will examine more closely each of those issues in the present chapter.

2. Shoreline Availability for Public Use

The ownership and use of shoreline recreation resources on a national basis was first documented in a 1954 survey conducted by the National Park Service.[2] That study found that almost every attractive seashore area from Maine to Mexico that was accessible by road had either been developed, acquired for development, or was under consideration for its development possibilities. At the time of that report, only six and one-half per cent of the Atlantic and Gulf Coasts were in federal and state ownership, and not all of this was devoted to recreational purposes. Noting this and the fact that there were still many large tracts--undeveloped due to their inaccessibility--that could satisfy future recreational needs, the Service recommended a vigorous program of public acquisition aimed at increasing the proportion of publicly-owned shoreline to fifteen percent. In 1962, the report to Congress by the Outdoor Recreation Resources Review Commission (ORRRC)[3] provided an opportunity to assess

2. U.S. Dept. of the Interior, <u>Our Vanishing Shoreline</u>, Washington, D. C. (1954).

3. George Washington University, <u>Shoreline Recreation Resources of the United States</u>, U.S. Outdoor Recreation Resources Review Commission Study Report No. 4, Washington, D. C. (1962).

the progress that had been made to that point, and the
results were disappointing.

A mileage summary of the detailed tidal shoreline and
recreation shoreline of major coasts of the United States in
1960 is shown in Table 3. The 28 contiguous coastal states
have nearly 60,000 miles of shoreline, of which about
one-third (21,700 miles) is considered suitable for recreation according to U.S. Coast and Geodetic survey

Table 3. Mileage of Tidal and Recreational Shoreline of
the United States (1960)*

Shoreline Location	Detailed Tidal Shoreline	Total Recreation Shoreline	Public Recreation Shoreline
Atlantic Ocean	28,377	9,961	336
Gulf of Mexico	17,437	4,319	121
Pacific Ocean	7,863	3,175	296
Great Lakes	5,480	4,269	456
Total	59,157	21,724	1,209

* Figures shown are in statute miles. Alaska and Hawaii
excluded.

Source: ORRRC Study Report No. 4, Shoreline Recreation Resources of the United States (1962), at 11.

criteria.[4] Of this recreational shoreline, there are 4,350 miles of beach, 11,160 miles of bluff, and 6,214 miles of wetland.[5] With respect to ownership in 1960, the figures presented in the table indicate that less than two per cent of the total shoreline was in public hands for recreation, while only about 5.5 per cent of the recreational shoreline was government-owned. On the entire Atlantic Coast, only 336 miles of shoreline were publicly-owned for recreation, a mere three per cent of the total recreational shoreline. Yet, this coast contains the population concentrations of the sprawling Northeast megalopolis and Florida. In the densely settled North Atlantic and Middle Atlantic Regions, there are 5,912 miles of recreational shoreline, of which 5,654 miles were under private or restricted public control; hence, 97 per cent of the shore in 1960 was inaccessible to the general public.

The most recent data available on the status of public recreational shoreline is provided by the National Shoreline Study, authorized by Congress in 1968 and

---

4. These criteria include: (1) the existence of a marine climate and environment; (2) the existence of an expanse of view at least five miles over water to the horizon from somewhere on the shore; (3) location on some water boundary of the United States. Id., at 11.

5. A beach is defined as a wide expanse of sand or other beach material lying at the waterline and of sufficient extent to permit its development as a recreation facility without important encroachment on the upland. Bluffs are characterized by banks or cliffs, immediately landward of a narrow beach, which vary in height from a minimum of several feet to mountainous elevation. Wetlands consist of either tidal or non-tidal marsh. Id., at 12.

completed by the U.S. Army Corps of Engineers in 1971.[6] A
mileage summary of the shoreline surveyed, together with
amounts of public ownership and public recreational use, is
shown for 1970 in Table 4.   While these data seem to
indicate substantial increases in public opportunities in
some regions, there are definite problems of interpretation
and   comparison   with   data   presented   in   previous

Table 4. Mileage of Erodable and Recreational Shoreline of
the United States (1970)*

Shoreline Location	Total Erodable Shoreline	Publicly Owned Shoreline	Public Recreation Use
Atlantic Ocean and Gulf of Mexico	27,680	6,260	2,130
Pacific Ocean	4,650	1,240	790
Great Lakes	3,680	650	370
Total	36,010	8,150	3,290

* Alaska and Hawaii excluded.

Source: U. S. Department of the Army, Corps of Engineers,
Report on the National Shoreline Study, Washington, D. C.
(1971), at 43-44

6. U.S. Department of the Army, Corps of Engineers, Report
on the National Shoreline Study, Washington, D.C. (1971).

reports.[7] The most important difficulty arises from the uncertain relationship between shore ownership to shore use. Much of the shoreline reported as used for public recreation may actually be in private ownership and thus susceptible to the increasing trend of private owners to restrict public access as demands increase. Furthermore, data on public ownership is not disaggregated to indicate how much of the public land is devoted to recreation purposes. While government acquisition programs during the 1960's have undoubtedly increased the supply of public recreational shoreline somewhat,[8] data from other sources seems to indicate that the percentage of public ownership for recreation remains low. For example, the major public

---

7. The problem is one of criteria used to define shoreline type and usage. For example, the Corps study excluded littoral areas not exposed to erosion by waves and currents. Total U. S. Shoreline (Alaska and Hawaii excluded) by this measure is 36,010 miles, versus 59,157 miles of tidal shore as cited by the ORRRC. A similar discrepancy exists with respect to beaches, with the Army Corps citing 11,970 miles and the ORRRC 4,350 miles. The difference stems from the fact that the Army Corp was interested in any beach capable of erosion, while the ORRRC dealt only with those capable of supporting recreation. Finally, no data is presented in the Corps report on the extent of the total shoreline that is suitable for recreation.

8. Coastal areas developed and administered by federal agencies now include 40 operated by the National Park Service (13 national parks and monuments, 9 national sea-shores and lakeshores, 28 historic areas); and 91 maintained by the National Wildlife Refuge System (20.4 million acres for management of migratory birds and other wildlife). See National Council on Marine Resources and Engineering Development, Marine Science Affairs--A Year of Broadened Participation, Washington, D.C. (1970).

shoreline additions since 1960 in the North Atlantic region have been the Cape Cod, Fire Island and Assateaque National Seashores, totalling 112 miles of coastline. Of this total, 53 miles was already in public hands, so that a net total of 59 miles were added to the public domain through federal acquisition.[9] Over this same period, private recreational development grew rapidly. It is estimated that, by 1970, almost 70 per cent of the total recreational property values along the ocean and Great Lakes coasts was accounted for by shorefront homes.[10]

In order to put the foregoing discussions in proper perspective, it would be useful to calculate the total carrying capacity[11] of the type of shoreline most popular for recreational use -- a beach. Assuming an average beach width above water of 50 feet, and allocating 100 square feet of space per person, the total U.S. beach mileage considered suitable for recreation by the ORRRC could accommodate roughly 11.5 million people. If 10 per cent of

---

9. North Atlantic Region Water Resources Study Committee, North Atlantic Regional Water Resources Study, Appendix N (1972), at 108.

10. Council on Environmental Quality, Environmental Quality--First Annual Report, Washington, D.C. (1970).

11. These assumptions are derived from the calculations in George Washington University, op. cit. note 3 supra, at 13. For an extremely detailed economic analysis of resource carrying-capacity, see Fisher and Krutilla, "Determination of Optimal Capacity of Resource-Based Recreation Facilities," 12 Natural Resources J. 417 (1972).

the population uses the beach at any given time (in season), then it would take all of the U.S. beaches to handle the demands of the coastal population of 108 million. But the total beach shoreline is not available to the public, as public ownership is limited to a small percentage and public access to private lands is increasingly denied. As a consequence, much of the potential demand necessarily goes unmet.

3. Suitability Factors

The problem of limited shoreline availability for public use is complicated by the problems of pollution and erosion. Pollution has destroyed countless fish and shellfish areas and fouled beaches in and around every major coastal city. In Boston Harbor, many islands would offer excellent opportunities for a variety of water-related activities were it not for the poor water quality, due in part to high bacteria counts resulting from municipal sewage dumping and storm sewer overflow. Oil spills, pesticides, and industrial effluents have also taken their toll of valuable shoreline resources. The case of the death of Lake Erie is probably the most celebrated example of this serious problem. In some cities, high pollution levels force the closing of beaches during the peak summer periods. Yet the pressures on shoreline facilities near metropolitan areas are so great that frequently the waters, even in busy harbors, are still used for recreational purposes by those who cannot afford to go elsewhere, regardless of whether they are safe for body contact or not. This again points to the problem of the

inability of low income, less mobile groups to find
suitable coastal recreational facilities anywhere but in
the immediate vicinity of urban centers, where the
pollution problems are most severe, and where fewer beaches
are available and oftentimes inaccessible due to gross
overcrowding.

The second element contributing to the decreasing
supply of suitable coastal land is shore erosion, which is
often accelerated by improper land use that stems from a
lack of knowledge of the dynamics of beach areas. A recent
article entitled "America's Shoreline is Shrinking" points
out the seriousness of this problem:

> From Cape Cod to California, America's
> ocean shoreline is being cut and furrowed
> by erosion. Much of this is the result of
> the ceaseless action of waves and wind, a
> combination of forces as old as the sea
> itself . . . (an example is) the dramatic
> case of Cape May, New Jersey, a famous
> resort area which has lost a fourth of its
> land area to the combined action of wind
> and wave during the last 30 years or so.
>
> The State of Maryland loses about 300
> acres of valuable land every year along
> the shores of Chesapeake
> Bay . . . Sections of shoreline at Point
> Hueneme, California. . . have receded as
> much as 700 feet in ten years.[12]

In its National Shoreline Study in 1971, the Army Corps of
Engineers found that 25 per cent of the total U.S.
shoreline exposed to wave and current action was undergoing

12. Bunker, "America's Shoreline is Shrinking," Boston
Herald Traveler, October 18, 1970, at 23.

significant erosion.[13] Frequently, these natural forces are greatly abetted by man. Ian McHarg, in his book, Design with Nature, has pointed out the dangers that trampling dunegrasses, lowering the level of groundwater, and interrupting littoral sand drift pose to the stability of dune formations. He has this to say about such formations in New Jersey:

> The knowledge that the New Jersey Shore is not a certain land mass as is the Piedmont or Coastal Plain is of some importance. It is continually involved in a contest with the sea; its shape is dynamic. Its relative stability is dependent upon the anchoring vegetation . . . If you would have the dunes protect you, and the dunes are stabilized by grasses, and these cannot tolerate man, then survival and the public interest is well served by protecting the grasses. But in New Jersey they are totally unprotected. Indeed, nowhere along our entire eastern seaboard are they even recognized as valuable . . . Sadly, in New Jersey no . . . planning principles have been developed. While all the principles are familiar to botanists and ecologists, this has no effect whatsoever upon the form of development. Houses are built upon dunes, grasses destroyed, dunes breached for beach access and housing; groundwater is withdrawn with little control, areas are paved, bayshore is filled and urbanized. Ignorance is compounded with anarchy and greed to make the raddled face of the Jersey Shore.[14]

---

13. See Army Corps of Engineers, note 6 supra, at 18.

14. McHarg, Design with Nature, Natural History Press, Garden City, N.Y. (1969).

4. A Case Example

The critical magnitude of the supply situation with regard
to shoreline resources can best be demonstrated by considering what has been happening in the State of Maine in
recent years. Maine's varied and beautiful shoreline is
its greatest asset; the coastal zone includes ten per cent
of the total geographical area, 36 per cent of the
population, and 127 local government units. Forty per cent
of the wages in Maine are generated in this zone, while
sixty per cent of all recreational property and seasonal
residences are located there. Almost the entire coast is
steep, rocky bluff with occasional small beaches of gravel
or mud.   In many areas, deep water occurs close up to the
shore. The coast is very irregular with numerous coves,
inlets, small bays, and similar areas serving as harbors or
sheltered areas. The shore area is only slightly developed
with only 34 miles (or 1.4 percent of the coastline) in
public ownership for recreation; the primary uses over the
remaining 2,578 miles are private with some commercial
resort activity.   The shoreline is least suitable for
swimming and water sports since there are only 23 miles of
beach along the entire coast. The most suitable activities
are camping, hiking, boating, sailing, and sightseeing, for
which the 2,520 miles of ragged, rocky bluff shore provide
an ideal setting. However, public opportunities to engage
in these activities are severely restricted in many places
due to extensive private ownership of prime coastal
property.

     While pollution has caused serious problems with the
taking of shellfish, by far the most serious question

facing Maine with regard to its shoreline resources is the
large percentage of private ownership. In 1967, a land use
symposium organized at Bowdoin College by land consultant
John McKee pinpointed the issues relating to this question
and outlined the successes and failures of Maine's
governmental bodies in dealing with it. McKee and his
colleagues argued for a public right of access to unique
shoreline, not only to a "mudflat or a rundown beach, but
to a cliff and forest and cove - precisely the places that
are selling fastest today", and warned that "unless Maine
decides right now to control the promise of development,
Maine's greatest asset will have been squandered,
irresponsibly, and definitely."[15] Such warnings have been
given repeatedly over the last decade by professional
planners, newspaper writers, conservationists, and others
concerned with the rapid disappearance of Maine's precious
coastal resources into private control. In 1970, the
situation was discussed in a series of articles by Robert
C. Cummings in the Portland Sunday Telegram, which outlined
the results of a survey of real estate agents, developers,
town and city officials, and county courthouse records:

> While Maine debates the pros and cons
> of oil refineries, sulfur reduction
> plants and aluminum processing, a quiet
> revolution in land ownership continues
> which promises to bar all but the most
> affluent from our 3,000 miles of ocean
> frontage.
>
> . . . development has already progressed
> to the point where, regardless of what
> the state does, there is unlikely to be

---

15. Cummings, "The Late Great State of Maine," Portland
Sunday Telegram, August 30, 1970.

enough suitable ocean frontage to serve
Maine and its ever-increasing hordes of
summer visitors.

Our survey reveals that Maine's coast
has been sold, and that the buyers are
largely from out of state. Big blocks
remain in the hands of speculators and
developers, and while plans are being
made, Maine citizens are wandering at
will as before, fishing the rocks,
harvesting the crops of wild berries and
enjoying secret picnic spots.

But the pattern has been set.
Wildland that in some cases was sold for
unpaid taxes as recently as a decade and
a half ago is about to become sites for
luxury vacation and retirement homes with
shore frontage selling for up to $100 a
foot - or $20,000 for a 200 foot lot.

Maine has probably lost its chance for
signigicant public control over its 3,000
miles of coastline. Indeed, before the
end of this decade, it appears certain
that people will have to begin lining up
before dawn on most good summer weekends
if they want a spot at a public beach.

This conclusion seems inescapable.
Some waterfront state parks are already
turning away visitors by noon or earlier,
overall park usage is increasing at the
rate of 20 percent a year and State Parks
and Recreation Director Lawrence Stuart
says flatly that desirable coastal property has practically disappeared.

Campers frequently have to wait in
line all night for a campsite to become
available at Acadia National Park. Persons who just want to go to the beach for
an afternoon will soon face "sorry we are
filled up" problems.

Dalton Kirk, supervisor of the park
district that ranges from Eagle Island
off Harpswell to Pemaquid, notes that ad-

missions to Reid State Park at Georgetown are up 20 percent, despite the opening of a new park across the Kennebec River at Popham Beach.

Kirk says that already in his region the state parks provide the only opportunity for most people to get to the beach. But Reid State Park twice this season has been forced to turn away beachgoers when the nearly 900 parking spaces were filled to capacity.

And at Popham, cars are turned away almost every good Sunday afternoon by 1 o'clock . . .

The state has purchased another 25 acres of mostly beach front this summer at Popham, and Kirk believes the facilities there can be doubled eventually. But this adds only 25 percent to the region's park capacity and the number of visitors is growing at twice this rate. Kirk sees no possibilities of further expanding Reid State Park without destroying the naturalness of the area.

"We need to get any beach frontage that is left in Maine," Kirk says. But if and when the State decides to buy, it may find little property for sale.[16]

Much of the Maine coast is in out-of-state ownership, which averages 45 per cent in the area but reaches 75 per cent in many communities. Many real estate brokers reported that 80 per cent or more of their business had been with out-of-staters. This boom is related to all the

16. Id. See also, Cummings, "Where Went the Maine Coast," Aug. 16, 1970 and "Maine For Sale: Everybody's Buying," Aug. 23, 1970. Portland Sunday Telegram.

factors previously mentioned: increasing populations, growing prosperity, and better transportation such as the Maine turnpike and highway system that makes half the state's coastline no more than a three-hour trip from Boston. These factors, combined with the desire to get away from the metropolitan atmosphere, have led to the un-precedented demands currently placed on Maine's coastal real estate. As a consequence, "Maine residents, the greatest number of whom find the stakes too rich for their income, have found themselves shut off from the sea and the wilderness by out-of-state buyers who put up a sign before they put up a house."[17]

5. Concluding Remarks

The purpose of this section has been to provide a general picture of the national supply of recreational shoreline. While a detailed inventory was not included, it is possible to draw some general conclusions by looking at the overall situation.

The first statement we can make is that the shoreline of the United States has, in general, been relegated to private interests. Shore property is highly desirable for private recreational use and as long as it is available there will be people to buy it, regardless of the cost. This seemingly boundless demand for a spot by the sea has sent land values skyrocketing: the price per front-foot of prime oceanfront property is often in the $100-150 range; the cost of an acre on the waterfront will often

17. Sherlock, "The Best of Maine Lost to the Rest of Maine," Boston Sunday Globe, Sept. 20, 1970.

exceed $50,000; and even some relatively wild areas such as found in parts of North Carolina or Maine are presently in the hands of speculators and developers, who are assured of a fantastic profit in the not-too-distant future.

Equally significant pressures for development of the shoreline come from industrial and commercial enterprises. Economic growth in the coastal areas has proceeded so rapidly that over 40 per cent of all manufacturing plants in the U.S. are located within the borders of coastal counties. The Army Corps has reported recently that the same percentage (16%) of the shoreline surveyed is devoted to private non-recreational development as to private recreational development.[18] Some of these activities have a demonstrated need for accessibility to water, either for transportation or as an input to production. For example, tanker-oriented oil companies and chemical manufacturers require multi-fathom harbors, while paper mills, primary metal plants, and power stations require substantial water supplies in the course of normal operations. But there are also many industrial and commercial activities taking place on the waterfront -- especially in urban areas -- for which proximity to water is not an essential operational ingredient. The end result of all this private development is almost invariably exclusion of the public. Many nonrecreation uses deny recreational uses absolutely, since "the practical and aesthetic requirements of clean water, adequate land area, safety

18. U.S. Army Corps of Engineers, op. cit. note 6 supra, at 7.

and pleasant surroundings, and necessary recreation developments can rarely be assured in conjunction with commerce, industry, housing, and transportation."[19] In addition, the practice followed by many shore owners for years of permitting public access and use of beach and bluff areas is rapidly declining. As the numbers seeking recreational pursuits in these areas increase each year, many states are finding that their private owners are now limiting such activity to maintain their own privacy. Hence, as the demands increase, this one part of the accessible supply is actually decreasing. Again, the situation in Maine is typical:

> The mountains are still there, the Atlantic Ocean still crashes its surf onto the rocks as it has done since the Ice Age and there is still some wilderness. It's just a little farther away now - on the other side of the fence.[20]

A second major point to be noted is the present saturation of most publicly-owned facilities. On the Connecticut shore, where the recreation facilities are under strong demand pressures from the dense New York-Connecticut metropolitan area, local communities find it necessary to institute user fees, parking charges, and other discriminatory devices to preserve for the local residents what small amounts of shore are left open to the public. The situation is much the same near other population centers in New England. Beaches on Narraganset Bay, Cape Cod, and in the Boston Metropolitan region are jammed almost every

---

19. See George Washington University, note 3 supra, at 7.

20. See Sherlock, note 17 supra.

weekend in the summer, while the beaches farther north become more crowded each year as New Englanders search for new, less crowded, accessible recreational areas. This trend is evidenced by the marked increase during the past few summers in traffic patterns leading from Boston to the Southern parts of New Hampshire and Maine.

The third and final major issue in shoreline supply is the influence of pollution and erosion, often caused by heedless development in ecologically delicate areas. Pollution, usually most severe where people are concentrated in large numbers, has closed many city beaches and threatens numerous others. Erosion too has closed or destroyed beaches and presents a continuous threat, especially in places like Miami Beach, Florida, where some hotels are built almost right in the surf; or in Ocean City, Maryland, where houses are built as close as six feet apart for many miles along the shore.

So this is the overall picture of shoreline supply: most of the land is privately owned and developed and is becoming more restricted to public access as the demands grow larger; and what is left in public lands for recreation is either saturated by hordes of users or unavailable for use due to pollution or erosion, especially near large cities. All this is to say nothing of the future. While the demands grow at a breakneck pace, the supply, limited to begin with, increases gradually, if at all. How can we expect to satisfy the demands of the future when we are having trouble supplying that which is needed today? This serious shortage of shoreline recreational resources points to an immediate need to protect all the shoreline resources still available, and to look for ways to accelerate the move towards increasing supply. Since the logical first step in approaching this task is to understand how the situation came about in the first place, we will focus attention in the following chapters on the institutional arrangements that have surrounded the allocation of shoreline resources to competing uses.

Chapter 4

INSTITUTIONAL FACTORS I: THE ORGANIZATION OF ECONOMIC ACTIVITY

1. Introduction

The problem of shoreline recreation is one of a number of issues of national concern regarding the use of unique coastal resources. We are concerned because historical processes have apparently been under-representing certain important social values while over-representing others. Public beaches have not been sufficiently provided while private development has mushroomed; water qualtiy has not been maintained as industrial and municipal wastes have made sewers out of many estuaries; and certain ecologically-important wetlands have not been protected from indiscriminate dredging and filling for residential or commercial use. The purpose of this and the following chapter is to provide a conceptual framework within which problems of this sort can be defined, their causes identified, and alternative proposals for solution evaluated. The framework essentially will comprise an analysis of the institutional mechanisms, both economic and political, which govern the allocation of any scarce resource among competing uses, with specific attention to the shoreline recreation question.

2. Efficiency and Equity as Goals of Resource Allocation

Saying that resources have somehow been misallocated implies that there exists some <u>optimal</u> allocation of resources that

---

1. While the system that allocates resources in this country is primarily economic and political, the law cannot be ignored as a forceful influence on the organization of allocative activity. The legal dimension and its relationship to the discussion in the present chapter will be developed fully in Part Two of this report, at p. 85 et seq.

is consistent with the overall values of society. While
this "social optimum" is impossible to determine in practice, it is quite useful to deal with in principle when trying to develop an understanding of the allocative system.
And integral to the notion of optimality are the concepts of
efficiency and social balance, which must be given clear and
well-defined meanings.

Efficiency and social balance are important concepts because there is only a limited amount of resources available
to our society. Limited resources include labor, technology, and natural resources, all of which are allocated to
the production of a wide variety of economic "products",
which are nothing more than whatever society find desirable
(physically, psychologically, aesthetically, or otherwise).
Public beaches can be thought of as "products" in this
sense, along with automobiles, television sets, health care,
and other familiar goods and services. Since resources are
limited, the total of all products that can be produced is
also limited. And since there is a ceiling on the amount of
products that might be available, the amount of each product
that society gets depends on how much of all the others it
desires. So, in other words, there are many combinations of
products that society might have, but the total level of
production is limited by the supply of resources. When we
succeed in achieving the total production possible given the
resources at our disposal, we are being efficient; and when
this production is distributed among goods and services in
accordance with aggregated social values and prevailing notions of equity and fairness, then we are also being social-

ly-balanced.[2] These concepts are illustrated in Figure 1, which depicts what is known as a production-possibility curve for a hypothetical economy in which only two products using coastal land resources are available to society -- electric power and outdoor recreation. The curve represents the maximum level of production possible given the limi-

Figure 1. The Production-Possibility Curve for a Hypothetical Two-Product Economy Based on Shoreline Use

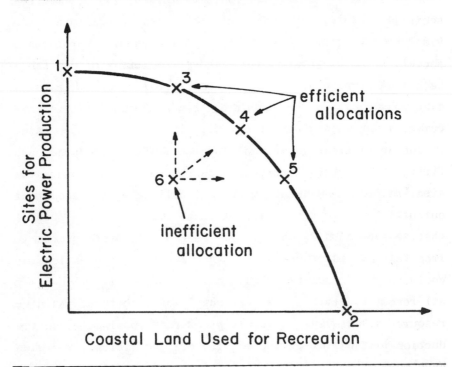

tations of the resource base, and each point on the curve
represents a different ratio of production for the two products. If no coastal land is devoted to recreation, we can
have a lot of power plants (Point 1); if no power is generated, the entire shoreline can be used for recreation; and
between these two extremes, there exist many production combinations (Points 3,4,5, etc.) of the two products. If society is efficient in its use of resources, the total output
of the two-product economy will lie somewhere on the production-possibility curve; and if the resource allocation is
socially-balanced, the relative amounts of each product provided by the economy will correspond to the relative value
society attaches to them. So, if resource allocation is to
be optimal, the economic system must operate on the production-possibility curve, and at a particular point on the
curve.

Two observations may help to clarify this analysis.
First, note the distinction between efficient and inefficient allocations.. When efficiency is attained (i.e., total
output is on the curve), having more of one product requires
that less be had of the other. If society wanted to move'
from Point 5 to Point 4, the gain in sites for power plants
could only come at the expense of recreation areas, since
all resources are being used to capacity. An inefficient
resource allocation, on the other hand, lies inside the production-possibility curve, and this implies that we could
have more of one product without reducing the amount we can
have of the other one. Point 6 represents inefficiency
since a more judicious application of resources could move
society toward any point between Point 3 and Point 5, i.e.,
we could have more power sites or recreation areas or both

without giving up any of either. If we assume that society always prefers more of a given product to less, then the movement from inefficient to efficient points makes us better off! The second observation of importance is that, while all the points on the curve represent efficient resource use (since total output is achieved), only one is optimal since society attaches priorities to each point depending on the relative amounts of each product it desires to have. At Point 3, there will be more power plants and fewer recreation areas than at Points 4 or 5. The optimal point represents that combination of products that would be produced if social value structures were perfectly articulated and weighed. But if for some reason certain social values are misrepresented, it is possible for resources to be allocated efficiently yet result in a distribution of products that is not reflective of social needs and values. For example, the economy may provide the efficient production combination of Point 4, even though society may value having the additional recreation areas and fewer power plants of Point 5. Efficiency without social balance is sub-optimal.

A more realistic production-possibility curve would actually be a multi-dimensional surface, a complex representation of the possible combinations of all available products. Within this context, we can think of public recreational uses of the coastal shoreline as desirable products to which coastal land and water can be allocated, along with other products (energy, waste disposal, private housing, industrial goods, etc.) that represent other aspects of social well-being (e.g. jobs, health, etc.). However, the concep-

tual goals of efficiency and social balance remain un-
changed. Public policy must be directed toward achieving
optimality, i.e. efficiency in production together with the
most desirable balance between the different dimensions of
well-being. But what are the instruments of public policy?
What are the institutional arrangements that society relies
upon to organize its activities and direct them towards optimality? In the United States, we rely on two interdepend-
ent decision-systems: A free-enterprise, competitive market
economy; and a representative democracy form of government.
Historically, we have exhibited a strong cultural preference
for market mechanisms in the allocation of resources, with
governmental action to correct for market imperfections.
Since our discussions in Chapters Two and Three lead us to
believe that these allocative processes have misallocatated
shoreline recreational resources, we must now discuss why
this has happened.

3. The Private Market

In every situation where finite resources are utilized to
satisfy needs that are almost infinite, there must be a
means of setting priorities. The private market is the primary mechanism through which we exercise the choice among
the combinations of products that might be provided, thus
determining the allocation of resources.

In a perfectly competitive market, aggregated personal
values are translated into desired amounts of production
through the workings of the price-profit system. The price
mechanism brings about effective proportional representation
of individual values through the "vote" of the dollar. The

profit mechanism brings about maximum efficiency through the
flexibility of decentralized decision-making.   If certain
basic conditions are met, there will exist a set of market
prices such that the activities of profit-maximizing firms
and benefit-maximizing consumers who respond to those prices
will automatically direct the economic system into an efficient allocative position.[3] This is a powerful result. If
the market can co-ordinate itself through a complex series
of mutual adjustment   processes, without the necessity of
outside intervention, then efficiency is assured. This has
led many economists to advocate reliance on market processes
to the greatest extent possible; indeed, a good deal of
government activity is designed to maintain the conditions
necessary for markets to perform efficiently (i.e. control
of monopolies). Yet even the most loyal defenders of the
competitive market system admit that there are circumstances
in which assumptions and conditions are violated such that
markets fail to provide certain worthwhile outputs and
underproduce others.

Aside from assumptions with regard to the nature of business behavior and the "perfectness" of competition, there
are two criteria governing the efficacy of market performance:

> 1) All desired products must be priced, and
>   social values must be capable of articula-
>   tion through wilingness-to-pay a price.

3. For a more extensive discussion, see Arrow, "The Organization of Economic Activity: Issues Pertinent to the Choice
of Market vs. Non-market Allocation," The Analysis and Evaluation of Public Expenditures: The PPB System, Vol. 1 (U.S.
Gov't. Printing Office, Wash. D.C. 1969), at 47.

This price must reflect the total social
cost of lost opportunity, i.e. the value
for other uses that is given up when resources are applied to the production of
any particular product. For the economic
system to move towards optimality with
every transaction, the social benefits of
devoting resources to the production of
the product in question must exceed the
costs.

2) Information must be available at low
cost to both producers and consumers.
Producers need knowledge of available
technologies, demand, and the costs of
factor inputs. Consumers need to know
what goods are available and what their
characteristics are. Both need to know
the relevant set of prices. In some instances, information might be scarce,
costly to collect, unreliable, or hard to
understand and evaluate without special
training.

Markets fail when the above criteria are not satisfied, and
this happens under certain circumstances. For example, the
transaction costs of organizing a fully-informed market may
be excessive. Costs are always attached to the collection
and dissemination of information regarding the terms surrounding transactions; and when these costs are too high,
the existence of the market is no longer worthwhile.[4] Markets also fail when the characteristics of certain goods and
services make them inherently unsuitable for provision by a
private enterprise system. The classic examples of this
situation occur in relation to the use of common-property
resources such as air. For people whose primary use of the
air is for breathing, clean air is a desirable product. For

---

4. Id. at 60.

others, such as the operators of a steel mill, the air is
also useful as a receptacle for gaseous wastes. However,
its use for this purpose has side effects on the breathers
of air, and these effects give rise to external costs. In
order for a market to assign priorities to the conflicting
uses, it must be possible to attach a price to the use of
each unit of air based on the magnitude of these costs. But
this is infeasible. First all all, pricing demands the exclusion of non-buyers from the use of the product; but con-
sumption of air by one person does not diminish or preclude
its availability to others. Secondly, prices must reflect
total social costs; yet how does one determine the amount of
damage done to a large and diffuse population over a long
period of time? Even if individuals could be excluded from
use or damages measured, the transaction costs of doing
these things would be enormous. Therefore, when prices do
not exist for products such as clean air, markets will tend
to overcommit resources to the production of other products,
thereby foreclosing the opportunity to allocate some of
those resources to more valued (but misrepresented) uses.
Products that are subject to market failure are sometimes
referred to as "public goods", and their provision necessarily entails some form of collective (governmental) action
since the economic system, left alone, will tend to produce
too many private goods and not enough public ones.

Before proceeding, one other aspect of private market operations should be noted. Even when the criteria for effective market performance are satisfied and efficient resource allocations are induced, this efficiency may not be
socially optimal. This is because the outcomes of market
transactions reflect the distribution of income in society.

Goods and services are provided by the market in conformance
with relative social desires, but only insofar as the participants are able to pay. But ability to pay frequently does
not correspond to the value society places on having certain
products. Therefore, even though the market can bring about
efficiency, it makes no claim for achievments regarding social balance. This, too, may give rise to the need for collective action.

   The provision of public goods through collective action
raises many issues well beyond the scope of this paper.[5]
Suffice it to say that the political processes of government
have imperfections of their own which stand as obstacles to
the achievement of optimality in the allocation of resources. At this point, it is appropriate to turn to an
analysis of the allocative system as it relates to shoreline
recreational resources, while the shortcomings of certain
forms of governmental action will become abundantly clear in
Chapter Five.

4. Market Allocation of Shoreline Recreational Resources

The private market is ill-suited for the allocation of recreational resources for public use; it fails in two respects. First, public recreation as a product does not lend
itself to the necessity of pricing. Consider, for example,

---

5. For detailed discussions of the role of government in relation to the economic system, see the collection of articles by leading economists in The Analysis and Evaluation of
Public Expenditures: The PPB System, especially "Part I:
The Appropriate Functions of Government in an Enterprise
System", (U.S. Gov't. Printing Office, Wash. D.C. 1969), at
13, et seq.

the difficulty in trying to determine the value of a scenic bluff or a sand beach to the regional public. Conceivably, a developer could provide coastal roadways with scenic vistas, or beaches with parking facilities and bath houses, and charge user fees. But the uncertainty in setting a fee based on the willingness-to-pay of a diverse public, coupled with the possibility of little or no short-term return on a large investment, make this highly unlikely. Even if the public could be polled to determine their preferences for shore recreation, the transaction costs of gathering such information could be prohibitive. Also, there is no guarantee that the information would be accurate, since people tend to misstate their preferences for economic goods depending upon whether or not they think they will be provided anyway. Thus, the need for elaborate and perhaps impossible studies to determine demand functions without the benefit of observing a market provides a serious obstacle to the provision of beaches or other facilities through private initiative.[6]

A second reason for market failure is that the shoreline shares in the common-property characteristics of the

---

6. A number of attempts have been made to apply economic theory to the evaluation of recreation benefits. For example, variability in travel costs has been used to identify a structural demand equation for an outdoor recreation site in the absence of ordinary market prices. See Clawson, "Methods of Measuring Demand for the Value of Outdoor Recreation", Resources for the Future Reprint No. 10, Washington, D.C. (1959). In general, the state of the art of such techniques is low and subject to a number of serious limitations. For example, the approach described above is suited to demand estimation for remote resource-based sites and not for population-based facilities in urban areas. For a general discussion, see Fisher, "Economic Theory and Recreation Benefit Evaluation," Marine Technology Society Ninth Annual Conference, (September, 1973).

land-sea zone, i.e. the aesthetics, unique climate and physical makeup, wealth of biological life, etc. As one commentator has noted:

> . . . The land component of lake/bay re-
> sources perhaps possess no more com-
> mon-property traits than does any land
> that can be plotted and deeded. However,
> when resource attributes of lakes and bays
> are considered, either singly or collect-
> ively, as the environment, the pervasive-
> ness of common-property characteristics
> will constrain the process of converting
> those resources into public goods and ser-
> vices.[7]

What this means is that, in the absence of any effective articulation of their value for public uses, resources such as the coastal shoreline will be overcommitted to those uses for which there does exist some mode of value-expression (i.e. a market price). These uses frequently entail highly capital-intensive development, such as industry, housing, commerce, and private recreation (beach clubs, private marinas, etc.). For example, the development of the shore as vacation home sites provides an immediate and well-defined return on investment. The same is true for other forms of private commercial or industrial development on the shore, since markets exist whereby the value of the resource to these enterprises can be articulated. Public recreation, on the other hand, ranks low on the capital-intensive scale; its value to the public is diffuse, costly to collect, and possibly unquantifiable. One commentator has summed up the situation as follows:

---

7. Craine, "Institutions for Managing Lakes and Bays," 11 Natural Resources Journal 519, at 524 (1971).

> (Recreation) occurs in an economic matrix
> that must be viable if continual degrada-
> tion is to be avoided. A recreational in-
> dustry must support the resident popula-
> tion or there will be pressure for nonre-
> creational industrial and commercial deve-
> lopment which in turn will reduce the re-
> creational potential. Unplanned recrea-
> tional developments, such as have charac-
> terized the past, do not result in an at-
> tractive coastal zone, satisfaction for
> the vacationing public, or a viable re-
> creation-based economy.[8]

In the absence of a properly-functioning market for public
recreation, the recreation industry described above cannot
develop.

While market failure presents a compelling rationale for
government intervention in the shoreline allocation process,
there is an additional source of justification. It is possible that even a properly-functioning market would, as
Craine has put it, "progressively limit to the higher income
classes the benefits arising from shoreline access."[9] This
conflicts with the expanding notion of recreation as an in-
alienable right, and of recreational resources -- especially
unique environmental ones -- as something all people should
have equal opportunities to enjoy regardless of income or
place in life. Typical of such sentiments were these words
of Lawrence Frank, in his report to the ORRRC on trends in
American living:

---

8. Ketchum, ed., The Water's Edge - Critical Problems of the
Coastal Zone, M.I.T. Press (1972), at 87.

9. Craine, op. cit. note 7 supra, at 520.

> A new slogan, declaring that recreation
> is the fifth freedom that we now urgently
> need to gain and enjoy the other four
> freedoms, might elicit a nation-wide re-
> sponse and a reaffirmation of our tradi-
> tional goals and historic aspirations.
>
> Seen as an indispensible, vitally im-
> perative need in the great movement for
> human conservation, we can say that oppor-
> tunity for outdoor recreation today is al-
> so an undeniable human right in a demo-
> cracy . . . no one should be deprived of
> outdoor recreation through which individu-
> als can make human living more significant
> and fulfilling, more conducive to the
> realization of their human potentialities
> and attainment of our enduring goal
> values.[10]

We can easily conclude from these observations that shoreline recreation for the public has every right to be considered a "public good", since an unfettered market would
allow the bids for private development to far outstrip those
for public use. This in fact is exactly what has led to the
supply situation described in the previous chapter. The
question that presents itself now is: Why has governmental
action failed to represent the interests of the public in
the shoreline?

This we shall deal with in the following chapter.

---

10. Frank, et al., Trends in American Living and Outdoor Recreation, Outdoor Recreation Resources Review Commission
(ORRRC) Study Report No. 22, Washington, D.C. (1962), at
231.

INSTITUTIONAL FACTORS II: THE ORGANIZATION OF
POLITICAL ACTIVITY

1. Introduction

While private market mechanisms are relied upon as the essential ingredient of the allocative system, they operate
within the broad legal and political constraints established by government. In this chapter, we will examine how
the organization of political activity affects the allocation of recreational resources in the coastal shoreline.
This organization consists of a large and diverse group of
governmental units at federal, state, and local levels, who
exercise some form of jurisdiction or control over varying
amounts of coastal property. Theoretically, these governmental units are in the position to effect policies that
could move the overall allocative process towards a
socially-optimal use of the shoreline. But we shall see
that politcal controls, for a number of reasons, also have
the potential to perpetuate inefficient resource utilization.

One problem common to all levels of government is a financial one. Historically, governments have sought to acquire public recreation resources through purchase or condemnation.[1] With land prices going up between 5 and 10 per
cent annually, and with lands suitable for public recreational use appreciating at a considerably higher rate , the
costs of wholesale resource acquisition are often well be-

1. See Chapter Eight infra, at p.139
2. See generally, U.S. Bureau of Outdoor Recreation, A Report on Recreation Land Price Escalation, Washingtion, D.C.
(1967).

yond the reach of many state and local economies. Furthermore, the costs of acquisition are only one part of the
overall fiscal picture. Beaches must be maintained and policed, with transportation facilities provided for access;
an increased influx of recreationalists might cause congestion and create additional demands for municipal services;
and the property tax base itself would be reduced by taking
prime waterfront property off the tax rolls. All of these
could be financially burdensome to state and local governments, especially in light of pressing needs for housing,
education, institutions, health care, and the whole range
of public services. A related problem is the conspicuous
absence of reliable methodologies for assessing the
socio-economic value that results from recreation-related
public expenditures.[3] While the costs of providing public
recreational facilities are abundantly clear, the benefits
may be intangible and unquantifiable. As a result, recreational needs often occupy positions of low priority on
state and municipal budgets, even to the extent that funds
necessary to match federal appropriations may not be
available.

While fiscal difficulties are often important   factors
that serve to inhibit effective collective action, they are
not so significant as the other common nemesis of all government activity, i.e., "the stifling effect of jurisdictional boundaries which, by a curious osmosis, permits the
diffusion of problems throughout the region, while blocking

3. See Chapter Four supra, note 6, at p. 68.

any corresponding flow of governmental responsibility."[4] This points to the natural consequences of fragmented political control over a resource such as the
shoreline, which is obviously no respecter of jurisdictional boundaries. Prime recreation areas are irregularly
distributed throughout most regions, and ever-increasing
leisure time and mobility bring increasing numbers of recreationalists to any richly-endowed location withing an expanding radius of urban centers. So while the problems
transcend local and even state borders, the responsibility
to deal with them has not been fixed due to the absence of
any logical place in the conventional government structure.
Almost by default, then, the local communities have been
left to control in an uncoordinated fashion the allocation
of resources that are of regional importance. And as one
might expect, there are orderly forces at work which cause
local decision-makers to act irresponsibly with respect to
the regional interest.

2. Decision-Making at the Local Level

Through the powers of zoning, subdivision control, acquisition, eminent domain and the like, municipal governments
are in the best position to encourage uses of the shoreline
most consistent with the general welfare. But the particular economic and political context within which local governmental units make decisions about shoreline use can lead

---

4. Perloff and Wingo, et al., Trends in American Living and
Outdoor Recreation, U.S. Outdoor Recreation Resources Review Commission Study Report No. 22, Washington, D.C.
(1962), at 84.

to inefficient allocation on a broad scale.[5]   We have already seen how the uneven distribution of prime recreational shoreline property places heavy demand pressures
from the region on specific communities, making their coastal property more valuable than some neighboring towns not
similarly "blessed" with good beaches or whatever. Yet, in
the absence of any mechanisms to articulate this regional
value, the municipality is free to use its powers[6] on
behalf of purely local objectives. The difficulty with
this situation is that municipalities are in general
willing to accept localized benefits when the costs are
distributed throughout the region, but, conversely, are not
willing to incur costs in order to provide benefits that
accrue to the region as a whole.

    This can best be illustrated by looking at the
decision-making process involving some coastal zone project, perhaps a power plant project. Let us first dis-
tinguish between two types of effects that might be associated with such a project -- direct and indirect.
Direct effects are those that accrue to the consumers or
users of the project: the user of the power supplied, the
former bathers on a closed beach, the swallowers of pol-
luted air, the viewers of marsh wildlife, etc. All of
these effects are felt by the local community and by the
regional society in general. Yet only those effects
(beneficial or otherwise) that accrue to the local populace
enter into the decision. The community may be willing to

5. See generally, Devanney, et. al., Economic Factors in
the Development of a Coastal Zone, MIT Sea Grant Project
Office, Report No. 71-1 (November, 1970).

6. See Chapter Ten infra, at p. 179.

give up beach or bluff property to have a power plant, but this may not be an optimal allocation of that resource on a regional basis. But the "votes" of the region are not counted -- only those of the local community affect the decision!

We might ask why a community might be willing to use this valuable property in such a way? The answer is that the local community within its particular economic and political context is also subject to a second type of effects, called parochial effects. These accrue to the suppliers of the resource that make the investment possible. Construction workers who build the plant will spend a substantial portion of their paychecks in the locale of the plants, certainly benefiting local merchants, doctors, and bar owners. These people, in turn, spend some of this money in the locale, and so on; this creates the traditional multiplier effect on local payrolls and retail earnings. Another very important factor is the broadening of the tax base that would result from new industry. For the local community, these benefits are very real; but considering the regional economy as a whole, parochial benefits are not net benefits, since those which are associated with one location will be about the same as those associated with an alternative site (barring large unemployment differentials).

Essentially, parochial benefits represent a transfer payment from one place in the economy to another, with no net benefit associated with the choice of site (even though there is a net benefit to the community chosen). Yet, parochial benefits can be overwhelmingly important to political bodies representing the local community, who can

rationally view a project in a very different manner from
the regional economy as a whole. The region and the local
community   both   feel   positive and   negative   direct
effects -- the community alone feels the parochial effects.
Thus any parochial benefits will persuade the community to
act in its perceived self-interest and approve the power
plant siting, with no consideration of the negative direct
effect to the region as a whole. This phenomenon has been
evidenced on the Maine coast, where much of the loss of
shoreline property to private development came with the
encouragement of state and local agencies and officials
eager for new taxable property and the jobs that developments generate. John McKee, the Bowdoin land use expert,
has said "it is surprising how many people will sacrifice
their coast. They say, if it'll bring in the tax dollar,
let's do it."[7]

Not all coastal communities have been incognizant of the
dangers of indiscriminate development, but those which have
preserved valuable resources for public use often try to
assert exclusive claims to their riches. Again, this is a
product of the forces of perceived self-interest:

> . . . What happens, in effect is that
> the resource rich communities find them-
> selves exporting tremendous volumes of
> free recreational services, frequently at
> a substantial social cost to themselves
> from the operation and maintenance of
> facilities and from the debasement of the
> recreation facilities to their own resi-
> dents. One reaction has been to wall out

7. Cummings, "The Late Great State of Maine", Portland Sunday Telegram, August 30, 1970.

> the problem by restricting the use of the
> resource: Public beaches confined to the
> use of local residents, stream banks, and
> wooded   areas   taken   over   by private
> 'clubs'. Carried to an illogical ex-
> treme, as such things sometimes are, the
> end result of this process is that a few
> have superlative opportunities for out-
> door recreation, while the great majority
> must   compete   for   the   services   of   a
> limited   supply   of   mediocre-to-poor
> recreation resources.[8]

Another problem with local level decision-making is its
high vulnerability to vested-interest pressures. A case in
point is that of the town of Harpswell on the Maine coast.[9]
In 1969, a Planning Board was created to assist the select-
men in dealing with the imminent threats of unrestricted
subdivision and other exploitation of the town's land. By
the 1970 town meeting, the Board and its consultant had
created a land-use ordinance aimed at developers whose
practices (insufficient soil surveys, inadequate sewage and
water systems, etc.) were not in the best interests of the
town.   At the meeting, Harpswell citizens who were opposed
to any form of planning argued vociferously against the
plan, and their emotional arguments were fueled by fears
created in part by the lobbying efforts of several local
developers and contractors (who supplied voters with bus
transportation to the meeting). As a result, the plan was
defeated and the Planning Board was abolished at the next
town meeting. As one commentator observed:

---

8. See Perloff and Wingo, op. cit. note 4 supra, at 86.

9. For a very interesting chronology of events, see Hutch-
inson, "Harpswell: What Went Wrong?", Maine Times, vol.
3, no. 2 (Oct. 9, 1970).

> Harpswell's future was on the line, and
> she stood defenseless before those who
> cared not for the common heritage of
> coastal land . . . with no planning board
> and no land use laws, Harpswell waits
> naked for the developers' invasion.
>
> What happened in Harpswell . . .
> could have happened in any Maine town
> that has not yet confronted the question
> of its destiny.[10]

At this point, we should emphasize one concept. While
local governments will tend to allocate resources of regional significance solely on the basis of local needs,
values, and pressures, this does not imply irrational behavior on their part. A town government is charged with
protecting the interests of the town residents, not the
public at large. In the case of coastal towns, the best
way to do this is to provide municipal beaches sufficient
to fill the needs of town residents who are not
shore-owners; charge discriminatory parking fees to protect
these beaches from overcrowding by "outsiders"; and leave
the remaining waterfront for private development to maximize the tax base. While this might be inefficient and inequitable from the regional standpoint, it serves to remind
us of the undue burdens that might be placed on both the
resource base and on the coastal towns under alternative
arrangements. Clearly there is a need for a broader per-

---

10. Id. Recently, Harpswell has begun to confront the
question of its destiny more seriously. Faced with two
large-scale residential developments, voters have approved
a moratorium that bans all subdivision, shopping centers,
and most other commercial developments until January 1,
1975, or until a comprehensive plan has been developed
and accepted by the town. Maine Times, July 13.

spective, but this perspective should not be allowed to arbitrarily preempt the legitimate concerns of the coastal
municipalities.

3.   State and Federal Programs

As   long   as there was plenty   of   shoreline   available   to
satisfy all the demands from competing private uses   while
still leaving ample opportunities for public use, there was
no perceived need for state or federal intervention in the
processes   of   the   market   and   local   political
decision-making.   Recreation was simply regarded as a
rather peripheral function of state and federal government,
along with conservation, aesthetics, protection of air and
water, and certain other goals which changed circumstances
or higher wisdom have now caused us to value quite highly.
As   late as 1935, the National Park Service surveyed the
Atlantic and Gulf coasts and found large stretches of unspoiled seashore areas suitable for recreation.[11] Since
the trends toward massive private development were beginning to take shape, the Service recommended that 12
areas comprising some 437 miles of prime beachfront be preserved as national parks. But by 1955, only one site had
actually been acquired, and all but one of the remainder
had gone into private and commercial development, along

---

11. See U.S. Dept. of the Interior, National Park Service,
Our Vanishing Shoreline, (1955).

with numerous other areas suitable for state reserves.[12]
Even then, the need for immediate action was not fully ap-
preciated, and private development continued to preempt
most of the shore. Prior to the 1960s, the states and the
federal government were not really cognizant of the coastal
zone as an environment separate from other regions of the
nation and in need of special attention. In the absence of
any long-range plans, these governments traditionally took
an incremental approach to satisfying increasing demands
for shoreline recreation. States typically reacted only to
short-term problems of supply, buying stretches of
shoreline needed to meet the expected demands over five- or
ten-year periods. While this was going on, potential sites
were privately bought to the point where, in many areas,
practically nothing remained to be developed.

In the early part of the 1960's, substantial funds began
to be appropriated for the purpose of securing additional
outdoor recreation opportunities for the public.[13] But
even these programs have been hampered in some ways, not
the least of which has been the bureaucratic process sur-

---

12. An example: In 1967 Miane citizens approved a $4 mil-
lion bond issue for park and coastal acquisition, even
though the legislation insisted on a provision prohibiting
the use of eminent domain powers. Yet, by 1970, though
prices in the meantime had doubled and quadrupled, and tens
of thousands of desirable acres had changed from open space
to luxury developments, the State Parks and Recreation
department has spent only $567,000, less than 12 per cent
of the money the voters authorized. And only part of the
purchases were coastal property. See Cummings, "The Late
Great State of Maine," Portland Sunday Telegram, August 30,
1970.

13. See discussion in Chapter Eight, infra, at p. 149.

rounding land acquisition.[14] In the first place, there is frequently a tremendous gap between authorizations and appropriations. Secondly, by the time the bureaucratic machinery grinds to the point of actual purchase (usually two to three years), considerable speculation and legal maneuvering further escalates the price of purchase or condemnation. The classic example is that of the Point Reyes National Seashore in California, originally estimated (in 1962) as costing a total of $14 million. By the time this money became available, speculation had doubled the price tag; and by the time Congress got around to authorizing an additional $5 million (in 1966), the price gap was wider than ever. As of 1968, the estimated total cost had risen to $58 million, more than quadruple the original figure!

Aside from cost factors, there are also problems with the very nature of certain federal grant-in-aid programs, which require that purchased parklands be made available to the general public and that projects fit into a comprehensive plan designed to meet basically regional needs. In the case of coastal towns with attractive beach shoreline, this may be the last thing they want to see happen. In the first place, the burdens of beach maintenance, traffic control, general policing, and the loss of prime waterfront property taxes may place undesirable strains on the local budget. Secondly, any decreases in the overall satisfaction that accrues to the local citizenry is certain to generate strong political forces at

---

14. For an excellent discussion of this dimension of the problem, see Whyte, The Last Landscape (1968), at 64-67.

state and local levels in opposition to proposed public
beach projects. The widespread municipal practice of
charging discriminatory parking fees to out-of-town users
lends weight to these arguments.

4. Concluding Remarks

We have found that the political activity which is relied
upon as a constant check and balance on the private market
has also contributed to the misallocation of coastal resources. For a number of reasons, government generally
has not put as high as value on public recreation as private owners have on waterfront land. High prices,
pressing social needs, and the difficulty of measuring intangible benefits all result in a planning procedure that
meets increasing demands on an incremental, piecemeal
basis. Consequently, many opportunities for acquisition of
valuable coastal acreage have been wasted in the face of
mushrooming development for private, commercial, and industrial use.

The second problem is a structural one, for even if each
community operates optimally within its own bounds, the
total shoreline allocation will not be optimal, due to the
lack of consideration of alternatives in which one community specializes in certain shoreline functions while
another specializes in some other activity. Purely local
planning may even lead to allocations that are worse than
an unrestricted market result, since whenever a local board
is faced with a development proposal, its first thought is
toward the secondary or parochial benefits of the project:
the effect on local payroll and retail earnings, broadening

of the tax base, etc. Yet, these benefits are not net benefits, but transfer payments from some other part of the economy.

The tendency is great to place the entire blame for ineffective collective action to meet public shoreline recreation needs on the shoulders of local government. But to do so obscures the underlying problem affecting all levels of government, i.e. the historical bias against planning in general, and against regional (or statewide) planning in particular. While the merits of planning are fairly debatable as a general alternative to decentralized markets for purposes of resource allocation, there is little doubt that -- in the shoreline case -- the absence of any effective methodology for the long-run provision of public facilities by government has clearly contributed to the shortage we face today.

This concludes the discussions of the social and economic nature of the shoreline recreational problem. What remains to be explored at this point is the legal dimension, for it is the law that will help shape and condition policy alternatives to alleviate the shortage of public opportunities on the coastal zone. For this, we now turn to Part Two of the report.

Part II

LEGAL ASPECTS OF SHORELINE FOR THE PUBLIC

Chapter 6

THE LAW OF THE SEASHORE

1. Introduction

In any society, the integrity and orderly conduct of economic and political processes depend on the law, which is best viewed as a process of creating, maintaining, and restoring an equilibrium in social affairs.[1] Through the legal system, social values and moral attitudes crystalize into constraints and guidelines for "right action" in decision-making, thus enabling members of society to calculate the consequences of their conduct. And when individual conduct is disruptive of the equilibrium in social order, the law functions to restore it. By making it possible to predict with assurance what others will do[2] and by guaranteeing the enforcement of this prediction through the powers of government, legal regimes interject an element of certainty in economic and political processes which facilitates voluntary transactions and arrangements. For example, a private market system relies on the existence of discrete "units" of production which an individual can possess to the exclusion of all others upon payment of a price. The legal system proscribes the violation of this "exclusion" principle

1. See generally, Berman & Greiner, The Nature and Functions of Law, at 28-36 (2nd ed., 1966).

2. As the venerable Oliver Wendall Holmes once asserted:

> The prophecies of what the courts will do, in fact, and nothing more pretentious, are what I mean by the law.

Holmes, "The Path of the Law" 10 Harv. L. Rev. 61, at 461 (1897).

through the construction of private property rights and their protection at law.

When referring to shoreline resources in a technical sense, it is clear that they are all part of an interrelated environmental system. The interactions of land, air and water form a complex mosaic of biological, chemical, and physical processes which must be dealt with in its entirety when managed from the ecological perspective. But the seashore has historically been managed from a social perspective, particularly with respect to the needs and desires of individuals, and the legal regimes governing activities in shore areas reflect this orientation. The maintenance of social order in the land-sea interface has required a legal delimitation between public and private rights which is artificial in the sense that it does not correspond to the "wholeness" of the environment. So in order to begin to understand the legal dimensions of the shoreline recreation problem, it is necessary to identify four distinct physiographic areas as comprising the "legal" seashore: 1) the water itself; 2) tidelands[3]; 3) submerged lands[4] other than tidelands; and 4) upland (dry) areas[5]. All of these are integral to most shoreline recreational activities, but in varying degrees.

---

3. The tidelands refer to the land between ordinary high and low tides, covered and uncovered successively by the ebb and flow thereof. See Blacks Law Dictionary, at 1656 (4th ed. 1951). For an extensive discussion from the technical side, see Shalowitz, 1 Shore & Sea Boundaries, at 84-89 (1962).

4. Submerged lands are adjacent to the tidelands on the seaward side and refer to those lands covered by water and below the low tide line.

5. Upland areas are adjacent to the tidelands on the landward side and extend inland from the ordinary high tide line.

For example, a day at the beach will generally entail
spreading a blanket on an upland sandy area, walking over
the tidelands and submerged lands, and swimming in the
water.   Similarly, a public boat launching facility would
require access and support facilities in upland areas,
wharves or ramps built on the tideland and submerged land,
and water on which to float one's craft.   While the recre-
ationalist considers these areas as a single entity -- the
seashore -- the law makes distinctions among them that are
very complex. The purpose of this chapter is to outline
these legal distinctions in connection with public recreational rights.

2. Public Ownership in the Seashore

The proximate source of public and private rights in seashore areas is ownership, an analysis of which must begin
with English common law. Sovereign authority over land, the
jus privatum or private title, was historically vested in
the Crown, and after the Norman conquest of England, the
King extended this authority to the sea and the lands beneath it.[6]   Since the original source of most land titles
in England was a grant from the Crown[7], it thus became possible for the title or other exclusive rights in any portion
of the seashore to be conveyed by the King to individual
subjects. By the time of the Magna Charta, private owner-

---

6. See generally Angell, A Treatise on the Right of Property
in Tidewaters and in the Soil and Shores Thereof (1st ed.
1826); Farnham, Waters and Water Rights (1904).

7. See 3 American Law of Property, s. 12.1 (Casner ed.
1952).

ship under this doctrine had proliferated to the point of substantial interference with commercial activities in the nation's waterways.[8] This initiated a gradual expansion of public rights in tidelands and navigable waters, which culminated in the application of the "public trust" theory to these areas by the English common law.[9] Under the public trust, certain public rights -- a _jus publicum_ -- were reserved[10] or held "in trust" for the common use and benefit of the public, even if proprietary title had been granted to individual subjects.[11] Such was the state of the English law at the time of the American Revolution; as a result, the thirteen original colonies, as independent sovereigns, succeeded to both the proprietary and "trust" interests held by the Crown[12], which they retained upon formation of the Union (subject to any rights surrendered to the Federal government by the U. S. Constitution[13]). In addition, each of the non-colonial states took on these attributes of sovereignty upon their admission to the Union, as required under the

---

8. Note, "The Public Trust in Tidal Areas: A Sometimes Submerged Traditional Doctrine," 79 _Yale L.J._ 762, at 765 (1970).

9. See Angell, op. cit. note 6 _supra_, at 33-34.

10. The rights so reserved were for navigation and fishing. See _infra_, at pp. 98-99.

11. See Farnham, op. cit. note 6 _supra_, vol. 1, at 165-172.

12. Shively v. Bowlby, 152 U.S. 1, 14 Sup. Ct. 548 (1894); Martin v. Waddell, 41 U.S. (16 Pet.) 367 (1842). See also Stone, "Public Rights in Water Uses and Private Rights in Land Adjacent to Water" 1 _Water and Water Rights_ 179, at 194-195 (Clark ed. 1967).

13. Id. See also discussion _infra_, at p.96.

"equal footing" provision of the U. S. Constitution.[14] In a long line of cases beginning in 1842[15], the U. S. Supreme Court confirmed state ownership of the tidelands and submerged lands beneath navigable waters, and it established that these lands are to be held in trust for the people of the respective states.[16] Furthermore, it is clear that the rights in tidelands under navigable waters within state boundaries are essentially a matter of state law[17], and it is generally understood that title to these beds gave the state the right to control the use of the overlying waters.[18] In sum, then, early American law held that each state owned the title to tidelands and lands under navigable waters within their respective boundaries and controlled them -- together with the waters -- subject to a public trust. The title to upland areas, of course, remained within the realm of purely proprietary interests. At this point, three questions present themselves: What are the boundaries within which state ownership/trusteeship applies?

14. For an extensive discussion, See Leighty, "The Source and Scope of Public and Private Rights in Navigable Waters," 5 Land and Water L. Rev. 391, at 414 et seq. (1970).

15. These cases are cited in Stone, op. cit. note 12 supra at 192 n. 61.

16. Id. at 195, notes 76-78. This of course does not preclude conveyance by the state, so long as the "trust" is upheld. See infra, at p. 97 et seq.

17. Shively v. Bowlby, 152 U.S. 1 (1894); Barney v. City of Keokuk, 94 U.S. 324 (1876); Pollard v. Hagan, 44 U.S. (3 How.) 212 (1845).

18. See Sax, Water Law, Planning and Policy, at 294 (1968).

What is the definition of navigability for purposes of title
determination? And what is the scope of the rights derived
from ownership and protected under the trust? These must
all be examined insofar as they relate to the shoreline recreation situation.

With respect to boundaries, the first issue is to determine the line between seaward state ownership and landward
ownership by private littoral owners. i.e. where does the
tideland end and the upland begin? In 1935, the Supreme
Court held that the common law rule normally applicable is
the mean of all high tides over a considerable time, and
this is the federal test.[19] A number of states, however,
have chosen not to follow this rule, and have designated the
low-water mark as the appropriate line[20]; other states
sometimes apply rules which extend the boundary landward beyond the high-water mark.[21] The second boundary issue concerns the seaward limits of state sovereignty. Between 1947
and 1950, a series of cases in the Supreme Court established
coastal state boundaries as the low-water mark of the

19. Borax Consolidated Ltd. v. Los Angeles, 296 U.S. 10, at
26 (1935).

20. Massachusetts (Great Colony Ordinance of 1647, ch. 53,
s. 3); Maine (Sinford v. Watts, 123 Me. 230 (1923)); New
Hampshire (Midd v. Hobbs, 17 N.H. 524 (1845)); Delaware
(Harlan & Hollingsworth Co. v. Paschall, 5 Del. Ch. 435
(1882)); Pennsylvania (Palmer v. Farrell, 129 Pa. 162
(1889)); Virginia (Va. Code Ann. s. 62.1-2 (1968)); Georgia
(Ga. Const. art. I, s. 6).

21. Louisiana (La. Civ. Code Ann. art. 451); Texas (Luttes
v. State, 159 Tex. 500 (1958)); In Washington, the mean high
tide has been equated with the vegetation line. See Harkins
v. Del Pozzi, 50 Wash 2d. 237 (1957).

seas.[22] This caused a storm of controversy, which resulted
in the enactment of the Submerged Lands Act of 1953[23], which
quitclaimed to the states title to the beds of the marginal
seas along a belt extending three miles (or three marine
leagues in the case of Texas and the Gulf coast of Florida)
seaward of the coastline.[24] These submerged lands and their
overlying waters were thus, in effect, added to the tidelands as subject to the sovereign control of the state.

The other class of submerged lands in addition to tidelands and lands beneath the marginal sea includes the beds
of internal waters, i.e. waters lying on the landward side
of the territorial baseline. According to the common law
rule, title to these submerged lands depends on whether or
not they are "navigable".[25] The federal test, as handed

22. U.S. v. California, 332 U.S. 19 (1947); U.S. v. Texas,
339 U.S. 707 (1950); U.S. v. Louisiana, 339 U.S. 699 (1950).

23. 43 U.S.C. secs.1301-15 (1970).

24. In subsequent litigation, the coast line applicable to
each state was held to be the baseline of the territorial
sea as adopted by the Convention of the Territorial Sea and
the Contiguous Zone (Geneva, 1958). See U.S. v. California,
381 U.S. 139 (1965).

25. In a number of jurisdictions, state title extends to
tidelands that are non-navigable. See Baer v. Moran
Brothers Co. (mudflat), 153 U.S. 287 (1894); U.S. v. Turner
(bay) 175 F2d. 644, 647 (5th Cir. 1949); Roberts v.
Baumgarten (creek) 110 N.Y. 380 (1888); Schultz v. Wilson
(marsh) 44 N.J. Super. 591 (1957); But see State v. Pacific
Guano Co. 22 S.C. 50 (1884) where title to the bed of a
non-navigable tidal creek was awarded to a riparian
proprietor. For a general discussion see Teclaff, "The
Coastal Zone -- Control over Encroachments into the
Tidewater," 1 J. of Maritime Commerce and Law 291, at
254-257 (1970).

down in the landmark Supreme Court case The Daniel Ball[26],
defines navigable waters as those which "are used, or are
susceptible of being used, in their ordinary condition, as
highways for commerce, over which trade and travel are or
may be conducted in the customary modes of trade and travel
on water."[27] This test is applicable to the issue of bed
title, since the beds of navigable waters within state
boundaries passed to the states upon their admission to the
Union as part of the transfer of territorial sovereignty
from the federal government. If the waters in question were
navigable by the federal test at that time, the beds automatically passed into state ownership.[28] It should be
pointed out that this federal test for navigability is mandatory only when bed ownership is at issue[29]; there are a
variety of other situations in which alternate forms of the
navigability criteria are applied at the state level.[30]

In applying the above considerations to the recreational
seashore, it seems clear that the public has rights attendant to state ownership and/or trusteeship in just about
every conceivable area touched by coastal waters. It is

---

26. The Daniel Ball, 77 U.S. (10 Wall.) 557, (1870).

27. Id. at 563.

28. See Leighty, op. cit. note 14 supra, at 421-422.

29. Id. at 433, 436.

30. These include the extent of public rights to surface use
under state law when beds are privately owned; correlative
rights of riparians in the same situation; rights of access
to the water by private riparians and the general public;
and certain specific rights under state laws. See Leighty,
op. cit. note 14, supra, at 398.

hard to imagine any coastal shoreline area (other than the upland) that is not either tideland, submerged land beyond the baseline of the territorial sea, or land beneath navigable waters.[31] Consequently, the issue of public rights in the seashore boils down to the following two questions: what is the extent of water-based rights derived from state ownership or protected from alienation through trusteeship? and how can the public welfare be represented in the upland areas? The remainder of this chapter will deal with the first of these issues, while the remaining chapters of Part Two will address the second.

3. Public Rights in Coastal Waters, Tidelands, and Other Submerged Lands

When title to tidelands or lands beneath navigable waters is owned by the state, the public almost always has the right to use the bed itself as well as the surface of the overlying waters for recreational purposes.[32] Even when waters are non-navigable for title purposes with the bed in private ownership, many states allow public surface use for recre-

---

31. This is especially true if one agrees with the assertion that navigable waters and their tributaries include "just about anything you can think of that flows." See Pearson, Significant Government Activities Concerning Coastal Waters and Estuarine Areas, LL.M. Thesis at Harvard School of Law, at 10, (May, 1972).

32. See Leighty, op, cit. note 14 supra, at 420. For a discussion of the precise scope of these rights under state law, see Leighty, "Public Rights in Navigable State Waters - Some Statutory Approaches," 6 Land and Water L. Rev. 459 (1971).

ation.[33] Whereas the waters off the coastal shoreline are generally navigable and thus imprinted with a public trust, the states have utilized this trusteeship "to maintain a public right of use for a wide variety of purposes, including not only navigation and fishery, but the whole spectrum of recreation uses as well."[34] Any such uses protected by state ownership or trusteeship are, of course, subject to the federal navigation servitude, which allows the promotion of navigation of the United States to supersede other interests.[35] But in the absence of any conflicting paramount national interest,[36] recreational rights in any given body of water are a matter of state law, and the states are free to develop their own tests for navigability, determine the disposition of state-owned lands, and regulate rights to sur-

33. Schoenbaum, "Public Rights and Coastal Zone Management," 51 N.C. L. Rev. 1, at 19 (1972). See also Comment, "Water Recreation - Public Use of 'Private' Waters," 52 Calif. L. Rev. 171, 172 (1964); Sax, op. cit. note 18 supra, at 264 n. 3.

34. Sax, op. cit. note 18 supra, at 294.

35. See Morreale, "The Navigation Power and the Rule of No Compensation," 3 Nat. Res. J. 1 (1963).

36. While it is possible that national supervision of the navigational aspects of recreational boating would be required under this doctrine as the number of pleasure boats increase, we are here concerned primarily with recreation activities taking place on or near the shore. In this case, paramount national interests are hard to envision. See Leighty, op. cit. note 14 supra, at 439-440.

face use.[37] Of these, it is the express conveyance or grant of state-owned tidelands to private parties which poses the greatest potential threat to public recreational rights. By the same token, it is the trusteeship associated with such areas that presents the greatest opportunities to preserve these public rights.

We should re-emphasize the point that there is no general prohibition against state disposition of trust properties, as long as the interests of the public are safeguarded or furthered by the purpose of the disposition.[38] In its landmark decision in <u>Illinios v. Illinois Central Railroad,</u>[39] the Supreme Court commented upon the constraints imposed by the trust:

> The State can no more abdicate its trust over property in which the whole people are interested, like navigable waters and soils under them, so as to leave them entirely under the use and control of private parties, except in the instance of parcels mentioned for the improvement of the navigation and use of the waters, or when parcels can be disposed of without

---

37. The Supreme Court has held that these powers are inherent attributes of sovereignty in the respective states. See U.S. v. Texas, 339 U.S. 707, at 716-717 (1950); U.S. v. Oregon, 295 U.S. 1, at 14 (1935). If any states "choose to resign to the riparian proprieter rights which properly belong to them in their sovereign capacity it is not for others to raise objection." Barney v. City of Keokuk, 94 U.S. 324, at 338 (1876).

38. See cases cited in Stone, op. cit. note 12 <u>supra</u>, at 197 n. 83, 84. For an extensive discussion of the trust theory, see Sax, "The Public Trust Doctrine in Natural Resource Law: Effective Judicial Intervention," 68 <u>Mich. L. Rev.</u> 411 (1970).

39. 146 U.S. 387 (1892).

> impairment of the public interest in what
> remains, than it can abdicate its police
> powers in the administration of govern-
> ment and the preservation of peace.[40]

Within these broad guidelines, the court made it clear that
it was left for the states to define the extent of public
rights in trust properties,[41] (i.e. the tidelands and lands
beneath navigable waters). While a few states are guided by
statutory law on the subject,[42] the common-law is the primary
means of identifying the scope of rights protected under the
trust.[43] And since the trust principle was inherited from
the English common law along with state ownership of tideland
and lands beneath navigable waters, this is the logical
starting point in the search for public recreational rights in
these areas. In England, the oldest and most completely protected public right in tidelands is that of navigation,[44] and

---

40. Id. at 453.

41. Id. at 452.

42. See note 20 infra, p. 92.

43. "What is a violation of the trust is an ad hoc judicial
determination depending on the facts of the particular case
and the extent of the public trust according to state law."
Schoenbaum, op. cit. note 33 supra, at 17. For an extensive
discussion of state law in the tidelands, see Garretson,
The Land-Sea Interface of the Coastal Zone of the United
States: Legal Problems Arising Out of Multiple Use and
Conflicts of Private and Public Rights and Interests. (U.S.
Dept. of Commerce Clearinghouse No. PB-179-428, September
1968).

44. "Of all the public trust rights, navigation is the only
one that has remained unchallenged and rigorously enforced
from Roman times to the present." Note, op. cit. note 8
supra, at 781.

public easements have been upheld for closely related activities such as anchoring.[45] The right of the English public to
non-navigation uses of tidelands that have been conveyed to
private owners was extensively discussed and settled in 1821
in Blundell v. Catterall:[46]

> The case directly involved the crossing
> of plaintiffs tideland to gain access to
> the sea for bathing, but it led to an ex-
> tensive discussion of the relative rights
> of a private owner and a person without
> littoral ownership but who asserted a
> general public right. A majority of the
> judges held that the public has no gener-
> al right to stroll, bathe, or linger on
> the beach, but there was general agree-
> ment that members of the public could use
> privately owned tidelands for passage or
> access to the ocean for the purpose of
> fishing.[47]

Thus, the English public's rights in the tidelands were limited to navigation and fishing, with passage generally allowed when connected to these rights. The bathing case was
again considered in 1904 in Brinkman v. Matley,[48] where the
judges, though sympathetic, relied on the doctrine of res
adjudicata[49] in holding that the earlier deliberation had
been too thorough to be reexamined.

---

45. Id., at 781, n. 73.

46. 5 B. & Ald. 268 (1821).

47. Stone, op, cit. note 12 supra, at 201.

48. 2 Ch. 313 (1904).

49. "It has been decided."

As American practice developed, it became clear that navigation, commerce, and fishing were the baseline rights protected under the trust theory.[50] These rights are upheld even in states which recognize private interests to low-water. In Massachusetts, the Great Colony Ordinance of 1647 reserved for the public the rights to navigation, fishing, and fowling in tidelands granted to littoral owners.[51] In Connecticut, where ancient usage has given upland proprietors the right to occupy tidal flats, interference with navigation is prohibited.[52] The right to passage over the tideland is frequently upheld,[53] especially in connection with navigation and fishing,[54] though this right is

---

50. "....(the State's title to soils under tidewaters) is a title held in trust for the people of the State that they may enjoy the navigation of the waters, carry on commerce over them, and have liberty of fishing therein freed from the obstruction or interference of private parties." Illinois v. Illinois Central Railroad, 146 U.S. 387 at 482 (1892). See also Note, op. cit. note 8 supra, at 783.

51. The Colonial Laws of Massachusetts 91 (1887 ed. reprinted from the edition of 1672); See also Michaelson v. Silver Beach Improvement Assoc., 342 Mass. 251, 173 N.E. 2d 273 at 277 (1961).

52. "The only substantial paramount public right is the right of free and unobstructed use of navigable waters for navigation." Orange v. Resnick, 109 A. 864 at 866, 94 Conn. 573, at 580-581 (1920).

53. See e.g. Barnes v. Midland R. R. Terminal Co., 193 N.Y. 378, at 385-386, 85 N.E. 1093, at 1096 (1908); Jackvony v. Powel, 67 R.I. 218, 21 A. 2d 554 (1941); Adams v. Crews, 105 So. 2d 584 (Fla. 1958); See also Stone, op. cit. note 12 supra, at 201.

54. See Moore and Moore, The History and Law of Fisheries, at 96 (1903).

not universally recognized.[55] While rights other than the a-
forementioned have not historically enjoyed the same degree
of protection, the trust concept has more recently been expanded by courts and legislatures to include park and recreational uses in tideland areas. To begin with, navigation
has been construed to embrace the use of waters for boating
or sailing for pleasure in any kind of water craft.[56] Some
jurisdictions have recognized the right to camp or hunt on
the foreshore,[57] and one New York court has held that the
right of the public to use the foreshore for passing and
bathing "is open to no manner of doubt."[58] In Oregon, the
legislature in 1967 declared that the foreshore of the Pacific Ocean is owned by the state and is to be preserved as a
public recreation area.[59] South Carolina, in a recent report,[60] has declared a *prima facie* claim of title in its

---

55. See State v. Knowles-Lombard Co., 122 Conn. 263, 188 A.
275 (1936). In Massachusetts, passage is allowed only over
the water over tidelands without any use of the land under-
neath. See Frankel, Law of the Seashore, Waters, and Water
Courses - Maine and Massachusetts (1969).

56. Silver Springs Paradise Co. v. Ray, 50 F. 2d 356 (5th
Cir. 1931).

57. Allen v. Allen, 19 R. I. 114 (1895); Collins v. Gerhardt,
237 Mich. 38 (1926); Muench v. Public Service Comm., 261 Wis.
492 (1952). Foreshore as used herein refers to tidelands.

58. People v. Brennan, 255 N.Y.S. 331, 142 Misc. 225 (1931).

59. Portions of the foreshore disposed of prior to July 5,
1947, are exempted from this law. Ore. Rev. Stat. Secs.
390.610-.690 (1968).

60. South Carolina Water Resources Commission, South Carolina
Tidelands Report (January, 1970).

450,000 acres of tidelands in and adjacent to the navigable
waters of the state, which are to be "held in trust for and
subject to the public purposes and rights of navigation, commerce, fishing, bathing, recreation or enjoyment, and other
public and useful purposes..."[61] In California, the State
Attorney General allowed the City of Long Beach to use its
tidelands oil income to operate public beaches on granted
tidelands on the grounds that this was "a proper trust use
and purpose."[62] More recently, the California Supreme Court
declared that privately held tidelands are subject to a trust
that has traditionally included "the right to fish, hunt,
bathe, swim, to use for boating and general recreation purposes."[63] In Florida, boating, fishing, and bathing rights
in trust properties were recognized as early as 1919,[64] and
in Washington, there are statutory limitations on the sale of
certain parts of the foreshore in connection with public recreational interests.[65] Finally, a number of states have exhibited an increased awareness of the need to protect trust
rights in areas of potential recreational interest. The Attorney General of Georgia has announced the state's claim to

---

61. See Porro, "Invisible Boundary - Private and Sovereign
Marshland Interests," 3 Nat. Res. Lawyer 512, at 519 (1970).

62. 33 Cal. Op. Att'y Gen. 152.

63. Marks v. Whitney, 6 Cal. 3d 251, 491 P. 2d 374 (1971).

64. Brickell v. Trammell, 77 Fla. 444, 82 S. 221 (1919).

65. Wash. Rev. Code Ann. s. 79.16.170 - 79.16.171 (1962); Ch.
120, Wash. Laws 559 (1967).

its marshlands;[66] the Florida Code has been amended to include natural resource conservation under the public
trust;[67] the estuarine areas of North Carolina have been the
object of extensive study;[68] and a bill permitting a lateral
right of passage below the vegetation line has been introduced in the Massachusetts legislature.[69] All these
observations indicate that the public trust is a flexible
doctrine which can be applied to changing public needs. One
commentator has related the evolution of public rights in the
tidelands to the pressures of supply and demand:

> Fishing and passage over the shore
> were probably the uses for which there
> was the greatest public demand and ser-
> ious need at the time when the question
> of public rights was being determined in
> the various states. Since that time, the
> serious public demand for access to the
> sea has been expanded by the widespread
> pursuit of such recreational activities
> as water skiing, spear fishing, skin
> diving, and a much more widespread desire

---

66. Bolton, Legal Ramifications of Various Applications and
Proposals Relative to the Development of Georgia's Coastal
Marshes (March, 1970). Cf. Note, "Regulation & Ownership of
the Marshlands: The Georgia Marshlands Act," 5 Ga. L. Rev.
563 (1971).

67. Fla. Stats. sec. 253.122.

68. Rice, Estuarine Lands of North Carolina: Legal Aspects
of Ownership, Use, and Control (April, 1968). In North
Carolina, private owners of lands littoral to navigable
waters have rights to construct piers or wharves, but this
right cannot be used to interfere with the public right to
use navigable waters for recreational purposes. See Capune
v. Robins, 273 N.C. 581, 160 S.E.2d 881 (1968); N.C. Gen.
Stat. s. 146 - 12 (1964).

69. S.804 (1973).

to hunt, fish, swim, and sunbathe.

*   *   *   *   *   *

The principle that the public has an
interest in tidelands...and a right to
use them for purposes for which there is
a substantial public demand may be derived from the fact that the public won
a right to passage over the shore for
access to the sea for fishing when this
was the area of substantial public demand.

The law regarding the public use of
property held in part for the benefit of
the public must change as the public
need changes.[70]

4. Concluding Remarks

It seems clear from the foregoing discussions that public
recreational rights in the waters, tidelands, and other submerged lands of the coastal shoreline are, in most cases,
firmly established. The greatest degree of protection stems
from state ownership, while the interpretation of the public
trusteeship in these areas has frequently expanded to include
recreational rights. This is not to say that significant
threats of encroachment in the tidal zone do not still exist.
In fact, the trust concept often fails to prevent indiscrimi-

---

70. Stone, op. cit. note 12 supra, at 201-202. The words of
two prominent jurists are particularly appropriate in this
regard: "We may not suffer (the law) to petrify at the cost
of its animating principle." Justice Cardozo in Epstein v.
Gluchin, 233 N.Y. 490, 135 N.E. 861 (1922); "Political,
social, and economic changes entail the recognition of new
rights, and the common law, in its eternal youth, grows to
meet the demands of society." Brandeis, in "The Right to
Privacy," 4 Harv. L. Rev. 193 (1890).

inate disposition of tidelands and must be "shored-up" by various forms of regulatory control over potentially destructive activities.[71] With respect to the shoreline recreation situation, however, it is probable that the larger part of the problem of public rights stems from private ownership of littoral property <u>above</u> the high water line, i.e. in the <u>upland</u> of the seashore. Though the waters and submerged lands may very well be open to the public, the seashore cannot be effective as a complete recreational resource without the use of uplands held by shorefront proprietors. Since this use is seldom forthcoming these days, public exclusion has become the rule of the coastal shoreline:

> The littoral owner not only may for-
> bid public crossing of his land to the
> shore, but also....he has a private right
> to cross the foreshore to the water him-
> self. In this way subdivision projects
> form Beach Clubs or the like, with virt-
> ual claim of monopoly; an increase in
> privatism over communism which finds ex-
> pression in signs "Private Beach, Public
> Not Allowed."[72]

On this note, it is appropriate to turn to the following chapter, where a consideration of the legal principles applicable in upland areas will commence.

---

71. For an extensive discussion of both the trust concept and state jurisdiction over activities in the coastal zone, see Teclaff, op. cit. note 25 <u>supra</u>.

72. Wiel, "Natural Communism: Air, Water, Oil, Sea, and Sea-shore," 47 <u>Harv. L. Rev.</u> 425, at 452 (1934).

Chapter 7

COMMON LAW PRINCIPLES AND PUBLIC RECREATION RIGHTS

1. Introduction

It is often the case that, when issues of political sensitivity begin to emerge from the social mileau, it is the judiciary that fashions the initial policy response and paves the way for subsequent legislative action. This has been true to a certain extent with respect to the shoreline recreation situation, where courts in Texas, Oregon, California, Florida, and New York have applied a number of common-law principles to preserve public rights in upland areas of the seashore. The purposes of this chapter are to review these principles as well as the case law and related statutory provisions which have relied on them; and to outline recent developments at the federal level which these "beach cases" have prompted.

2. Prescription

Prescription is one means by which rights in real property can be acquired, and it is the principal legal theory governing the creation of public easements in privately-owned land. The doctrine holds that such an easement can be created through continuous, open, and adverse use of the land in question, without permission of the owner. In most states, prescription is authorized by statute, and the period over which adverse use must take place is frequently specified.[1]

---

1. In California, however, the public may not take prescriptive easements in land. See People v. Sayig, 101 Cal. App. 2d 890, 226 P. 2d 702 (1st dist. 1951).

In <u>Downing v. Bird</u>,[2] the Supreme Court of Florida set forth the typical elements necessary for the establishment of a prescriptive right in land:

> In either prescription or adverse possession, the right is acquired only by actual, continuous, uninterrupted use by the claimant of the lands of another, for a prescribed period. In addition, the use must be adverse under the claim of right and must either be with the knowledge of the owner or so open, notorious, and visible that knowledge of the use by and adverse claim of the claimant is imputed to the owner. In both rights the use or possession must be inconsistent with the owner's use and enjoyment of his lands and must not be a permissive use, for the use must be such that the owner has a right to legal action to stop it, such as an action for trespass or ejectment.[3]

Prescription has very recently been applied in a straightforward manner to a beach case in Florida, <u>City of Daytona Beach v. Tony-Rama, Inc.</u>[4] The defendant corporation owned a stretch of beach and operated a recreational pier extending across this property into the Atlantic Ocean. The dispute centered on the granting of a building permit to the defendant for the purposes of constructing an observation tower on the soft sand area adjacent to the pier. Claiming that the public had acquired a prescriptive recreational easement in the area, a group of citizens and taxpayers had

---

2. 100 So. 2d 57 (Fla. 1968).

3. Id. at 64-65.

4. 2 ELR 20511 (Dist. Ct. App. Fla. August 31, 1972).

won a judgement in their favor, which the appellant sought
to overturn. The court found that the public had actually,
continually, and uninterruptedly used and enjoyed the soft
sand area for a wide range of recreational purposes for over
twenty years; that the public's use was adverse under an apparent claim of right and without material challenge or interference by anyone purporting to be the owner of the land;
and that the city had maintained the area, policed the flow
of traffic and the parking of vehicles, and otherwise exercised the police power over the area for the general welfare
of its users. These circumstances fell well within the precedent of three earlier Florida cases, such that a finding
in favor of the public's right to a prescriptive easement
was readily forthcoming. In addition, the court ruled that
the city was empowered to exercise supervisory jurisdiction
over the area and to authorize the construction of lifeguard
towers, sanitation facilities, or other such structure not
inconsistent with the public easement.

The only other beach case which has relied upon the prescription theory is <u>Seaway Co. v. Attorney General</u>,[5] a landmark Texas case decided in 1964. Prior to this time, the
rule of law as established by the Texas Supreme Court in
1959 had been that fee ownership of the sandy areas of the
beaches of the state above mean high tide were for the most
part in private ownership.[6] This controversial ruling pre-
cipated the enactment by the legislature of the <u>Open Beaches</u>

---

5. 375 S.W. 2d 923 (Texas Civ. App. 1964).

6. See Luttes v. State, 159 Tex. 500, 324 S.W. 2d 167 (Tex.
Sup. 1959).

Act of 1959,[7] which declared a presumption that the public had a prescriptive right to use the beach seaward of the vegetation line, and authorized the Attorney General to defend this right.[8] In Seaway, the court utilized the statute only insofar as the mandate to the Attorney General was concerned,[9] although the clear legislative policy embodied in the Act undoubtedly affected the outcome. The Seaway Company owned a portion of the beach on Galveston Island, and had erected barriers to exclude the public from the upland dry sand area below the vegetation line.[10] The court ruled against the company in finding that the public had made continuous use of the beach over the requisite 10-year period according to statutory law; and that adverse use for roadway and recreation purposes had been establishment because "whoever wanted to use it did so....when they wished to do so

---

7. Chap. 19, Acts of the 56th Legis., 2nd Called Session (1959), as amended by Chap. 659, Acts of the 56th Legis., Regular Session (1965). Codified as Texas Rev. Civ. Stat. Ann., Art. 5415 d. V.A.T.S.

8. For a detailed discussion of the Act by its author, see Eckhardt, "The Texas Open Beaches Act," The Beaches: Public Rights and Private Use, Texas Law Institute of Coastal and Marine Resources, Conference Proceedings, at 7 (January, 1972).

9. The issues surrounding the declaration of the presumption of the public right will be discussed further infra, at p.139.

10. It is interesting to note that such exclusion did not become a common practice until after the 1959 decision (note 6 supra), because private landowners aparently had assumed all along that the beaches were owned by the public, having been used for at least a century prior to 1959. See Newman, "The State's View of Public Rights to the Beaches," The Beaches, op. cit. note 8 supra, at 12.

without asking permission and without protest from the land-owners."[11] In addition, the court was able to rely heavily on a number of roadway cases since the beach had long been used as a public highway.[12]

A third beach case which discussed the prescription theory but did not rely on it was State ex rel. Thornton v. Hay.[13] Here, the court refuted defendent's argument that the general public cannot acquire prescriptive beach rights because actions in ejectment or trespass cannot be brought against it. The court acknowledged this point but pointed out that public exclusion is possible through posting and fencing the land. Other arguments were similarly refuted, indicating again that the prescription doctrine can be effectively applied as a means of preserving public rights in private beaches, when the circumstances are appropriate.

3. Customary Rights

At the other end of the spectrum from the prescription theory, at least in terms of frequency of application, is the doctrine of customary rights, which holds that immemorial observance of a custom may accord it the force of law under

---

11. 375 S.W. 2d 923, at 936 (1964). The finding of adverse use was also used to justify a holding that a public easement has been dedicated. This will be discussed further infra, at p. 112.

12. See discussion infra, at p.114.

13. 254 Ore. 584, 462 P. 2d 671 (1969). However, the trial court ruling which was affirmed by the Supreme Court relied heavily on the prescription theory. No. 27-102 (Ore. Cir. Ct., January 3, 1969 -- unreported).

certain circumstances.[14] A custom is defined as a "usage or
practice of the people which, by common adoption and acquie-
sence, and by long and unvarying habit, has become compul-
sary, and has acquired the force of law with respect to the
place or subject-matter to which it relates."[15]   This doctrine has been revived for application to the beach case in
State ex rel. Thornton v. Hay,[16] where the Supreme Court of
Oregon specifically selected it over implied dedication and
prescription on the grounds that beaches, by virtue of their
unique character, deserve the special treatment that the
custom doctrine can provide.   The case involves a suit
brought by the state against a motel owner who had fenced
off part of the beach (to which he held title) beyond high

---

14. The circumstances providing the test for the custom
doctrine are as follows:
   (1) it must be ancient
   (2) right must be exercised without interruption
   (3) use must be reasonable and peaceable
   (4) boundaries of use must be certain
   (5) custom must be obligatory and not inconsistent
      with other customs or laws.
For a historical analysis of the doctrine, see Note, "Public
Access to Beaches," 22 Stan. L. Rev. 564, at 582 et seq.
(1970).

15. Blacks Law Dictionary 461 (4th ed. revised 1968).

16. No. 27-102 (Ore. Cir. Ct. 1969), affirmed on other
grounds, 254 Ore. 584, 462 P. 2d 671 (1969). In this case,
the court acted pursuant to an Oregon statute that was virtually identical to the Texas law discussed infra. See Ore.
Rev. Stat. secs. 390. 610-.690 (1968). However, as in the
Seaway case, the court did not pass on the constitutionality
of the statute, relying on common-law grounds as a basis for
the decision.

tide and below the vegetation line for use by motel patrons
only. In ruling against the defendant, the court found that
the public had enjoyed uninhibited use of the state's
beaches throughout its history, and this usage was sufficient to create a customary right of recreation that precluded the private owner from excluding the public.[17]

4. Dedication[18]

Dedication is generally defined as "the devotion of property
to a public use by an unequivocal act of the owner, mani-
festing an intention that it shall be accepted and used
presently or in the future."[19] To be complete, dedication
depends both on the intention of an owner to offer land or
some interest or easement therein as well as acceptance by
the public; and both of these can be either express or implied.   One commentator has summarized the concept as follows:

> Common law implied dedication comprises a
> system of judicially created doctrines
> governing the donations of land to public
> use. No formalities are necessary; con-
> duct showing intent by the owner to dedi-
> cate land and an acceptance by the public
> completes the dedication. Both intent to
> dedicate and acceptance may be implied

---

17. Id., at 673.

18. For an in-depth analysis of issues only touched upon
herein, the reader is referred to Note, "Public Access to
Beaches," 22 Stan. L. Rev. 564 (1970).

19. McQuillin, 11 The Law of Municipal Corporations (3d ed.
revised), sec. 302, pp. 627-630.

from public use. An owner's inaction may
be taken as evidence of acquiescence in
public use and thus of his intent to do-
nate the land. The public use itself may
be taken as evidence of acceptance.

Once the implicit offer has been accepted, the owner cannot revoke his dedication. The public cannot lose its rights
through non-use or adverse possession.
The public normally takes only an easement
by implied dedication, with the owner retaining the underlying fee; a few courts,
however, have found dedication of a fee
simple title in circumstances indicating
an intent to give such a title.[20]

Prior to 1964, a number of unsuccesful attempts had been
made to apply the dedication principle in beach situations.
In F. A. Hihn Co. v. City of Santa Cruz,[21] the court allowed
dedication of a roadway along a beach, both of which had
long been used by the general public for recreational purposes, but rejected the claim of dedication of the beach as
well. A similar result was arrived at in City of Manhattan
Beach v. Cortelyou,[22] apparently because beaches at the time
were considered in a class with infrequently-used lands such
as prairies and forests. Such lands were subject to an "open-lands limitation" which presumed that their owner had allowed public use under a revocable license, since it was
thought that occasional use would not be sufficient to put
an owner on notice of a public claim. The limitation was

20. See Note, op. cit. note 14 supra, at 573, text and notes
45-53.

21. 170 Cal. 436, 150 P. 62 (1915).

22. 10 Cal. 2d 653, 76 P. 2d 483 (1938).

generally relaxed in roadway cases, but for some ambiguous
reason the courts preferred to classify beaches with much
less frequently-used wildlands.[23] Evidently the courts felt
that the need for public beach areas could be adequately
fulfilled elsewhere and did not warrant unnecessary incur-
sions on private properties. In the 1960's, however, as the
shortage of public beach opportunities in many areas became
increasingly apparent, dedication came to be viewed from a
new perspective, and in Seaway Co. v. Attorney General,[24]
the principle was succesfully applied to a beach case for
the first time. In Seaway, the court found an intent to
dedicate by relying on the same evidence of adverse use that
it had used to establish a prescriptive easement.[25] In addition, the fact that the beach had long been used as a public highway[26]-- the most common context within which public
easements have been dedicated -- had substantial precedent-
tial value. The open-lands limitation was similarly laid to
rest in the 1969 Oregon case, State ex rel. Thornton v.
Hay,[27] where the trial court upheld the dedication of an

---

23. This issue is discussed fully in Note, op. cit. note 14
supra, at 579.

24. 375 S.W. 2d 923, at 936 (Tex. Civ. App. 1964).

25. See supra, at p. 109. While dedication and prescription
are theoretically distinct, the line between them was completely obscured in this case. See Note, op. cit. note 14
supra, at 577-578.

26. The beach had a history of roadway use extending back
over a century to when it was used as a stagecoach route.

27. No. 27-102 (Ore. Cir. Ct., 1969), affirmed on other
grounds, 462 P. 2d 671 (1969). See discussions supra, at
pp. 110-112.

easement and noted that heavy recreational use by the public over a 60-year period could hardly be construed as putting beaches in a category with other unimproved lands.

The next instances of beach dedication for public use were litigated in the California Supreme Court in 1970, which ruled on two similar cases, <u>Dietz v. King</u> and <u>Gion v. City of Santa Cruz</u>, in a single opinion.[28] In <u>Dietz</u>, a beach and its access road had been continuously used by the public for 100 years until 1959, when the King family attempted to discontinue this use. In <u>Gion</u>, the plaintiff sought a determination of his right to develop three parcels of oceanfront property which has been used for a number of years by the public and which had been maintained by the City of Santa Cruz for more than five years. The court granted recreational easements in both cases on the following grounds:

> ...common law dedication of property to the public can be proved either by showing acquiescence of the owner in use of the land under circumstances that negate the idea that the use is under a license or by establishing open and continuous use by the public for the prescriptive period. When dedication by acquiescence for a period less than five years is claimed, the owner's actual consent to the dedication must be proved...When, on the other hand, a litigant seeks to prove dedication by adverse use, the inquiry shifts from the intent and activities of the owner to those of the public.[29]

---

28. 2 Cal. 3rd 29., 84 Cal. Rptr. 162, 465 P. 2d 50 (1970).
29. Id., at 38.

Since adverse public use had been well-established in both
cases, the court was able to rely on the latter of these two
rationales while avoiding the problem of dealing with the
owner's intent to dedicate. As one commentator has noted,
these cases "helped render the distinction between an   easement acquired by implied dedication and one acquired by prescription almost nonexistent,"[30] in much the same way as the
Seaway case had done in Texas. Finally, the open-lands limitation was once again set aside:

> One of the most interesting aspects of the
> Gion case is its holding that there is no
> presumption that use of land by the public
> is by implied license of the owner.   Thus
> the implied license to use open lands ap-
> pears to have fallen to the passage of
> time in California.   Owners must now show
> affirmatively that they granted the public
> a license to use, or they must demonstrate
> that they have made bona fide attempts to
> prevent public use....
>
>   Thus, what Texas and Oregon have at-
> tempted to accomplish by statute   the
> Supreme Court of California has accom-
> plished in part by judicial decision.   In
> these three states, at least, the burden
> of proof is on the landowner to overcome a
> prima facie showing that the public has
> established a right to the use of the
> shoreline.31   (Emphasis added).

---

30. Comment, "Public Rights and the Nation's Shoreline," 2
ELR 10179, at 10188 (Sept. 1972).

31. Id.

Dedication of beaches has been used not only to validate claims of public use in favor of private owners, but also to enforce rights of the public at large vis-a-vis local residents. In Gerwitz v. City of Long Beach,[32] a 1971 ordinance was held invalid which restricted to local residents use of a municipally-owned beach that had been used by the public at large for over thirty years. The court found that there had been a complete and irrevocable dedication of the park to the public at large; that the intent of the city to so dedicate was manifest in its official actions; including supervision, maintenance, and the collection of admission fees; and that the element of acceptance by the public at large can be inferred from the use that was made of the beach over a considerable period of time.[33] Furthermore, the court suggested that when it is a municipality that is making the dedication, "the element of acceptance really is not required, or if the element of acceptance is to be insisted upon, it may be implied from the very act of dedication by the municipality."[34] Finally, the court held that when the city dedicated the property, it put itself in the position of holding that property subject to a public trust for the benefit of the public at large, so that it may not be diverted to other uses or sold without express legislative authority.[35] Since the facts in Gerwitz were such that

32. 330 N.Y.S. 2d 495 (1972).

33. Id., at 505.

34. Id., at 505.

35. Id., at 509.

the application of dedication theory was straightforward, further discussion will be confined to the public trust aspects of the case.

5. The Public Trust Doctrine[36]

As discussed in Chapter 6, the public trust doctrine has found application to the seashore insofar as the protection of public rights in the tidelands and lands below navigable waters are concerned. On the other hand, no broad trusteeship governs the upland portion of the seashore, since the general rule is that early land titles granted by the federal government to private individuals ran to the high water mark and included the dry-sand portion of the beach. The trust concept has, however, managed to creep ashore in some areas through a less direct route. As American practice in the environmental field has developed, the public trust has become a useful tool for the protection of parklands,[37] and beaches and other shoreline areas that have been purchased by government for public recreational use are clearly public parks. Trust properties of this sort are generally characterized by a three-fold limitation on the authority of government as trustee: (1) the property cannot be sold; (2)

---

36. For an in-depth analysis of the issues only touched upon herein, the reader is referred to Comment , "Public Rights and the Nation's Shoreline," 2 ELR 10179. See also Note, "Water Law - Public Trust Doctrine Bars Discriminatory Fees to Non-residents For Use of Municipal Beaches," 26 Rutgers L. Rev. 179 (1972).

37. See Citizens to Preserve Overton Park v. Volpe, 401 U.S. 402 (1971).

the property must be maintained for particular types of public uses impressed with the trust; and (3), the property
must be available for use by the general public.[38]   These
restrictions as applied to beach/park situations were reviewed in the previously-discussed case of Gerwitz:

> ...Public parks occupy a special position
> insofar as the public at large are con-
> cerned, and this is borne out by numerous
> expressions to that effect found in the
> decisions of this state.   (Citations
> omitted) Attempts to divert public park
> property to other uses have often been re-
> strained....
>
> The view that land which has been dedi-
> cated to use as a public park may not be
> diverted to another use or alienated finds
> support in the decisions of other states
> (citations omitted).[39]

As we have seen, the issue in Gerwitz was the exclusion of
non-residents from the use of a town beach, and this was invalidated on the grounds that the public trust protects the
rights of the public at large and not just the local populace. A similar ruling was applied to a New Jersey beach
case, Borough of Neptune City v. Borough of Avon-by-the-
Sea,[40] where non-residents of Avon-by-the-Sea were charged

---

38. See Sax, "The Public Trust Doctrine in Natural Resource
Law: Effective Judicial Intervention," 68 Yale L. J. 471,
at 477 (1970).

39. 330 N.Y.S. 2d 495, 2 ELR 20524 at 20528 (1972).   But see
Paepcke v. Public Building Commission of Chicago, 46 Ill.
2d 330 (1970), which allowed the construction of a school on
park lands that had been dedicated to public use, on the
grounds that legislative permission could be found in a number of broadly-worded statutes.

40. 61 N.J. 296 (1972).

higher user fees than residents for use of a municipally-owned beach area.[41] The purpose was to defray the municipal costs incurred through non-residential use, which was
alleged to have caused a $50,000 town deficit. A lower
court found that this was "cogent and compelling justification" for the establishment of disproportionate fees based
on residence,[42] but this was reversed by the New Jersey
Supreme Court. The court held that the upland area of the
Avon beach had been dedicated for recreational uses and that
"the public trust doctrine dictates that the beach and the
ocean waters must be open to all on equal terms and without
preference and that any contrary state or municipal action
is impermissible."[43] Thus, as in Gerwitz, the Avon decision
affirmed the right of non-discriminatory access to trust
properties; but the court in Avon apparently had a broader
interpretation of the scope of this concept:

> The court does not explain, however, why
> the right of access prevents municipal-
> ities from reasonable discrimination be-
> tween resident and non-resident beach
> users. A reasonable explanation is that
> the court has extended the common law no-
> tion that impediments to public trust
> property are impermissible.

41. In New Jersey, the question of absolute exclusion of the
public at large had been settled in 1954, when a trial court
in Brindley v. Borough of Lavallette invalidated an exclusionary ordinance on the grounds that New Jersey law forbids
discrimination among citizens. 33 N.J. Super. 344, 110 A.
2d 157 (Law Div. 1954).

42. 114 N. J. Super. 115, at 123, 274 A. 2d 860, at 865 (Law
Div. 1971). A 1950 New Jersey law had empowered coastal
boroughs to regulate their beachfront and charge reasonable
fees. N.J. Stat. Ann. s. 40:92-7.1 (1967).

43. 61 N.J. 296, at 309 (1972).

Under Avon, it appears an impediment
need no longer physically intrude upon
the trust property, nor need it be physical in nature. The imposition of a discriminatory fee constitutes an impediment.[44]

6. Prospects and Problems of the Common-Law Approach

The increased judicial protection of public rights in the
seashore represents the first constructive step towards
counteracting the erosion of public recreational opportunities in the nation's coastal shoreline. Through the application of a variety of common-law doctrines in the seven
"beach cases" discussed above, the courts of a few progres-
sive states have fashioned meaningful responses to the need
for recognizing the land-sea interface as a uniquely valuable environmental resource, deserving of special treatment.
These courts have exhibited a willingness to adjust the interpretation of traditional concepts to meet the challenges
of new situations in modern times. Some doctrines (prescription, dedication, public trust, custom) have been expanded [45] or revived, while others (open-lands limitations,
presumption of revocable license) have been narrowed according to their relevance to the issues at hand.

The common-law approaches described above seem to have
great potential for preserving existing opportunities for

---

44. Note, op. cit. note 36 supra, at 182-183.

45. By 'expanded' I mean that the courts have basically had
little trouble in overcoming relatively minor conceptual
problems occasioned by the application of these doctrines in
new and somewhat unconventional contexts.

public use of the shoreline. In Chapter 3, we noted that
the effective supply of public recreational resources was
being adversely affected by the increasing tendency of private owners to restrict access to seashore areas previously
open to the public, and by the municipal practice of excluding non-residents from the use of local facilities. These
trends could be reversed through widespread utilization of
the legal tools discussed herein; and it is also possible
that these same tools can be used to significantly increase
the availability of shoreline for the public. Before this
great potential can be realized, however, some serious difficulties must be overcome which threaten to preclude the
effectiveness of the common law approach as a tool of public
policy.

The biggest problem with recreation planning through ad
hoc judicial action is that it is not really planning at
all. This is because it is subject to much uncertainty, depending as it does on jurisdiction-by-jurisdiction and
case-by-case adjudication. With regards the former, it is
important to point out that the court decisions we have reviewed apply only in the respective states where the cases
were tried,[46] and even then the scope of some rulings has
not always been clear.[47] Courts in other states may not be

---

46. In New York, for example, a 1935 decision refused to
accept the customary right doctrine as a valid means of creating an easement for bathing in a private beach area. See
Gillies v. Orienta Beach Club, 159 Misc. 675, 289 N.Y.S.
733 (1935).

47. In Oregon, there is some question as to whether the
court's decision in Thornton applies to all state beaches or
only to the litigant's property. See Note, op. cit. note
18 supra, at 564.

so inclined to reinterpret or expand legal concepts like the
public trust, or to dispose of minor conceptual problems
like the adverse use requirement that a landowner have a
remedy at law (such as ejectment or trespass) that can be
applied to the general public. The landmark rulings in
Oregon and Texas were greatly aided by the existence of
state statutes[48] that clearly reflected legislative approval
of activities serving to protect the public interest in the
seashores. Most other coastal states, however, have little
or no statutory law on this issue, and have not otherwise
taken steps to reaffirm or protect to the fullest extent
rights which the public may have in littoral uplands.

With regards the case-by-case nature of the common-law
approach, there is the danger that scores of littoral property owners may feel sufficiently threatened by the apparent
trend in judicial attitudes to take steps to obviate the
possibility of legal challenge. If large stretches of previously open beach begin to be fenced off by private owners,
and if there is not prompt action to assert the public
right, the discontinued use that results may be sufficient
to obviate any enforcement of public use easements.[49] And
even when challenge is possible, the practicle difficulties

---

48. Ore. Rev. Stat. secs. 390.610-.690 (1968); Texas Rev.
Civ. Stat. Ann., Art. 5415 d., V.A.T.S.

49. "The problem of giving notice of the public claim becomes extremely severe when the public has remained silent
for many years after ceasing to exercise its easements.
More fundamentally, taking by public use may be justified
because the owner has in effect opened the door to the public; if no one complains for many years after that door is
closed, the original justification is lost." Note, op. cit.,
note 18 supra, at 579.

in bringing action to determine the public's right in every
stretch of beach may be prohibitive. An assistant attorney
general in Texas has described this problem as follows:

> It is often difficult to resolve whether
> [a public] right of use or easement has
> been established; this necessarily in-
> volves a question of fact for a jury de-
> termination. The enforcing official
> cannot merely show a barricade or ob-
> struction... but must prove further
> that the public in fact has acquired an
> easement to the area in question by rea-
> son of dedication, prescription, estop-
> pel, and continuous right. This is a
> difficult task, requiring much investi-
> gation and the expenditure of large sums
> of money. One must determine what use
> the public has made of the beach in the
> past, secure ancient documents to show
> the beach has been used by the public
> for many years and obtain witnesses to
> testify as to the nature of that use.
> This is an enormous undertaking.50

The above observations indicate that, while the recent
flurry of judicial attention to the shoreline recreation
problem is encouraging, it is fairly debatable at this point
to what extent the common-law approach can be useful in the

50. Newman, "The States View of Public Rights to the
Beaches", The Beaches: Public Rights and Private Use, Proceedings of a Conference sponsored by the Texas Law Institute of Coastal and Marine Resources, University of Houston,
at 11 (Jan. 1972). The Seaway case was described in this
article as a "massive production" which required five weeks
of jury trial and at least as much preparation. It is easy
to visualize how difficult it might be to establish public
rights through the doctrine of custom, since proof of public
use from the beginning of a state's history may be very hard
to come by.

long-run. Decision-making with regard to the allocation of
recreational resources   among   competing   private and public
demands must come through a rational, coordinated planning
process, one which is not subject to the myriad uncertainties of fragmented adjudication of individual cases. This
has raised the question as to whether there should be an attempt by federal legislation to bring some uniformity to
both the public policy regarding rights of shoreline access
and the means by which these rights can be established.
Such a national "boost" toward solving the shoreline for the
public problem has in fact been proposed in the form of the
National Open Beaches Bill,[51] which has been under consideration by the Congress since 1969. Essentially, this bill is
intended to facilitate and encourage the continued application of any common-law technique that might be relevant
within the legal context of each respective coastal state.
If enacted and allowed to stand, this legislation could be
extremely useful in broadening the base of litigation con-
firming public rights in the nation's shores. Thus the
overall success of the common-law approach is closely linked
to the success or failure of this bill, and for this reason
it is important here to outline its provisions and to consider some of its legal and practical implications.

---

51. H.R. 10394, S.2691, 93rd Congress, 1st Session, introduced by Rep. Robert Eckhardt (Sept. 19, 1973) and Sen.
Henry Jackson (Oct. 30, 1973). Rep. Eckhardt is the author
of the Texas Open Beaches Act, discussed supra. The full
text of the national bill is contained in Appendix B,
infra, at p. 251.

7. The National Open Beaches Bill[52]

The National Open Beaches Bill declares that the beaches[53] of the United States are impressed with a national interest, because they have traditionally been used in connection with marine transportation, commerce, and recreation. To protect this national interest, the bill provides that:

> The public shall have free and unrestricted right to use [the beaches] as a common to the full extent that such public right may be extended consistent with such property rights of littoral owners as may be protected absolutely by the Constitution.[54]

This statement embodies the concept that even though the fee simple title to littoral land is held by a private owner, public rights of access and use for recreational and other purposes may still exist and can be affirmed through judicial application of certain legal doctrines

---

52. For a complete discussion of the bill and its underlying rationale by its author, see Eckhardt, "A Rational National Policy on Public Use of the Beaches," 24 Syracuse L. Rev. 967 (Summer, 1973). See also, The Beaches, op.cit., note 50 supra, at 36.

53. A "beach" is defined in the bill as the area along the shore of the sea affected by wave action directly from the open sea. The sea "includes the Atlantic, Pacific, and Artic Oceans, the Gulf of Mexico, and the Carribean and Bering Seas, and the Great Lakes. H.R. 10394, secs. 201 (2), (3) (93rd. Cong. 1st. Sess., 1973). The beach is more precisely defined for a variety of situations in secs. 201 (3) (A), (B), 201(4), 201(5), and 201(8).

54. Id., sec. 202.

(prescription, dedication, etc.).[55] Towards these ends, the
bill authorizes the Attorney General of the United States
or a U. S. district attorney to sue in federal court to determine the existing status of title, ownership and control, in order to prevent any unjustifiable obstruction of
public rights which may be found to exist.[56] What this
means, in effect, is that since public rights to use
beaches are national in scope, the federal government--as
well as the states--is justified in taking legal action to
vindicate them,[57] as long as such action is consistent with
private property rights established under existing state
law.

---

55. See Eckhardt, op. cit., note 52 supra, at 972-973,980-
982.

56. H.R. 10394, sec. 203 states that "no person shall
create, erect, maintain, or construct any obstruction,
barrier, or restraint of any nature which interferes with
the free and unrestricted right of the public, individually
and collectively, to enter, leave, cross, or use as a common
the public beaches." To effectuate this provision, the bill
provides that "an action shall be cognizable in the district
courts of the United States without reference to jurisdictional amount, at the instance of the Attorney General or a
United States district attorney, to: (1) establish and protect the public right to beaches, (2) determine the existing
status of title, ownership, and control, and (3) condemn
such easements as may reasonably be necessary to accomplish
the purposes of this title." Id., sec. 204 (a).

57. It has recently been argued that the bill is beyond a
doubt constitutional as regards these provisions, i.e. both
as to the assertions of a federal interest in the openness
of beaches, and as to the authorization of federal suits to
uphold this interest. See Black, "Constitutionality of the
Eckhardt Open Beaches Bill," 74 Colum. L. Rev. (1974).
(unpublished as of this writing).

It should be pointed out at this point that property owner's rights, as determined by state law, could never be extinquished under the proposed federal law. Landowners whose titles provide the right to restrict or deny public access would not be affected; at the same time, owners whose titles do not provide that right would be left with all the property rights they ever possessed.[58] This question of whether or not private titles in beach areas are held subject to public rights is usually a matter of state law, but the difficulty is that the courts in most coastal states have never been squarely faced with the issue. The objective of the bill, then, is to foster the _clarification_ of existing state law through litigation.[59] And if the federal courts can legally assume juristriction in beach cases, then it is wholly approriate for them to rule in those areas where state law is clouded or has not yet reached.

It should not by any means be inferred from the above observations that the National Open Beaches Bill envisions un-

---

58. For a discussion of these points, see, "Remarks of Louis E. Reed, Jr.", _Congressional Record - Senate_, at 1884 (February 5, 1971).

59. "If the law were clarified through litigation, such could and in many areas would result in a holding that the public had retained its access to the beaches through a variety of legal theories ...The purpose of a federal law should be to facilitate this process... "Eckhardt, op. cit., note 52 _supra_, at 982. For example, in the wake of the _Avon_ decision in New Jersey, there is speculation that the public trust doctrine may find application to privately-owned shorefront areas heretofore thought well beyond the reach of the doctrine. See Note, op. cit., note 36 _supra_. See also Comment, op. cit., note 36 _supra_, at 10191.

ilateral action at the federal level. Section 207 of the bill states that, "in order to carry out the purpose of this title, it is desirable that the States and the Federal Government act in a joint partnership to protect the rights and interests of the people in the use of beaches." This spirit of cooperation is also reflected elsewhere in the bill. Section 208 places federal research and technical facilities at the disposal of the states to aid in the preparation of cases; section 209 authorizes grants to cover 75 per cent of the costs of planning, acquisition, or development of state projects designed to secure the right of the public to beaches;[60] section 210 authorizes financial assistance to states to develop and maintain transportation facilities necessary in connection with the use of public beaches;[61] and section 206 provides that all interests in land recovered through federal action shall be treated as subject to the ownership, control, and authority of the state in the same measure as if the state itself had acted to recover such interest.

Aside from declaring a national policy with respect to open beaches and establishing a federal machinery for litigation and financial assistance, the National Open Beaches Bill also specifies rules of evidence that are applicable in all litigation brought under its title. These are as fol-

---

60. To qualify for these grants, the state must be in compliance with relevant provisions of the bill and must have established adequate state laws to protect the public's right in beaches.

61. To qualify for these grants, the state must define and sufficiently protect public beaches by state law.

lows:

> (1) a showing that the area is a beach
> shall be prima facie evidence that the
> title of the littoral owner does not in-
> clude the right to prevent the public
> from using the area as a common;[62]

> (2) a showing that the area is a beach
> shall be prima facie evidence that there
> has been imposed upon the beach a pre-
> scriptive right to use it as a common.[62]

The practical effect of these provisions in the legal sense
is that they shift the burden of proof to the littoral proprietor to rebut the presumption that the public has established a right to make recreational use of the upland portion of the seashore. In considering the constitutionality
of this Congressional allocation of burden, one commentator
has recently concluded that all the elements that are looked
to as rational support for such a presumption are present in
the beach situation:

> It is unquestionable that the littoral
> owner, claiming the right to obstruct a
> beach and to make a beach his own, is far
> better positioned than the public can be
> with regard to access to the evidence
> concerning prior use. The question
> whether, on the whole, the beaches of
> America have been used by the public from
> time immemorial, is a question about
> general custom and social history,
> suitable for Congressional determination;
> if Congress in effect makes the determin-
> ation by enacting section 205, then no
> court would fault it unless it were clear-
> ly wrong. It seems very unlikely that evi-

---

62. H.R. 10394, sec. 205 (1), (2).

> dence could be produced to show generally
> that the custom as to our beaches has
> traditionally been one of private right
> and exclusion.[63]

These observations suggest that the constitutionality of the
rebuttable presumption established in the bill depends
wholly on the exercise of reasonable judgment on the part of
Congress. That the establishment of such a presumption is
reasonable depends to a large extent on whether there is
some rational connection between facts proven and facts
thought to be presumed. To establish such a connection, the
author of the National Open Beaches Bill examined all the
state cases previously described in this chapter, and found
that all have common elements which support the conclusion
that beaches are generally impressed with a public interest.[64]

In sum, it has been asserted that the enactment of the
National Open Beaches Bill is well within the purview of the
constitution; and that Congress should speak on the question

---

63. See Black, op. cit., note 57 supra. (Quote is based on
a tentative draft of this article, made available with permission of the author prior to its publication).

64. "All the cases cited which address the question of public access to the dry sand beach have important elements in
common: (1) the cases all culminate in protection of a public right, (2) they all rest upon a customary public use
from time immemorial or over an expanse of time sufficient
to ripen custom into a prescriptive right; and (3) they all
take into account the special character of the beach and the
public interest therein." Eckhardt, op. cit., note 52 supra,
at 980. See also Black, op. cit., note 63 supra. "If public suits invariably or even more commonly than not 'culminate' in an upholding of the public claim, then a rebuttable
presumption of the existence of the public right is plainly
rational."

of shoreline for the public for the following reasons:

> The passage of [the National Open
> Beaches Bill] would clarify federal pub-
> lic policy and would show federal recog-
> nition of a difference between ownership
> and the right of public use;... It would
> be most salubrious if an opportunity
> were given, as is done in [this bill],
> for the attorneys general of the states
> and of the United States to act together
> in seeking to achieve a common goal.
> The act would only accelerate the pro-
> cess of utilizing state theories for
> protection of their public beaches by
> declaring federal policy in their favor,
> by establishing favorable prima facie
> presumptions, and by bringing to the aid
> of the states all federal legal and
> technical expertise to establish the
> public right to use of ocean-front lands
> back to the vegetation line.[65]

8. Concluding Remarks

Prior to the foregoing discussion of the National Open Beaches Bill, it was argued that a number of uncertainties tend to inhibit the effectiveness of common-law strategies to regain shoreline for the public. If this federal law were to be enacted, however, it now appears likely that the most serious of these difficulties would be obviated. In the first place, a definitive statement of Congressional concern for public access to the shoreline would doubtlessly influence judicial determination on the issue, as the courts may become more receptive to suggestions that common-law concepts be reinterpreted to meet changing social objectives. Secondly, many of the practical problems associated

---

65. Eckhardt, op. cit., note 52 supra, at 985.

with numerous and costly litigation might be eliminated if the rebuttable presumption in favor of the public interest is upheld. For example, a littoral landowner who once tolerated public use could no longer take steps to terminate it in order to avoid the possibility of legal challenge to assert a public right. The very fact that he attempts to fence out the public would in itself be suggestive of a traditional public use, and would therefore support a presumption that the shore is impressed with a prescriptive right of common use. The presumption creates further disincentive for exclusionary action in that it shifts the burden of proof to the individual proprietor, who may not be so willing to go to the perhaps great expense of invalidating the public claims that may ensue. This is particularly true if some other landowner had previously tried and failed, thereby creating a precedent in the case law of the state. Consequently, it may not be necessary for the state's attorney general to bring a multitude of actions to cover large portions of the shore; one or two may be sufficient to appraise private owners of the attitude of the courts and the ability of the attorney general to enforce any public interest that might exist.

Having so arrived at a favorable assessment of the National Open Beaches Bill, there are some additional considerations that should be noted in connection with common-law approaches in general, and the proposed federal law in particular. First, it is possible that common-law doctrines--even with federal assistance--may not apply to a large enough portion of the total coastal shoreline to make a significant dent in the overall problem of public access. In some cases, there may be no factual basis for arguing the existence of a public right, as private title rights which exclude public use may be firmly established as a matter of state law. In other cases, the nature of the shoreline itself may not be supportive of the concept of traditional public use, which is best applied to beaches and perhaps not so well to other types of recreational shore-land. For example, in areas such as northern New England or the Pacific Northwest, where rocky bluffs often dominate the coastal landscape, the legal concepts of dedication or prescription may find little to commend them.

A second potential problem with the common-law approach is that posing the recreational issue solely in terms of public vs. private rights may lead to inequity in the de-termination of who benefits and who pays. The _Avon_ case, discussed earlier, provides a perfect example. While it is reasonable to expect the public at large to have access to all municipal beach areas, it is also reasonable that town residents should not be required to shoulder a disproportionate share of the costs of maintenance. But there is little room for consideration of the latter of these issues when the public trust doctrine is applied as it was in _Avon_, where the question as to what is a reasonable fee and what is an exclusionary fee was not directly addressed by the court. A similar issue arises with respect to conflicts between public use and no use at all. By no means is every beach area in the U.S. best suited to un-limited public use; in some cases, the overall public in-terest may best be served by denial of unfettered access. Yet environmental factors may have only a tangential affect

66. See _supra_, note 36, at p. 118.

on court decisions where the primary question is whether a public or private right should prevail.

These observations are not in any way meant to argue that the common-law approach cannot play an important role in connection with the shoreline recreation situation. They are merely illustrative of the fact that no single policy tool, by itself, is likely to be sufficient to solve the problem of inadequate public access. In some situations, common-law techniques will be appropriate; in others, they will not. The National Open Beaches Bill, then, should be assessed not for its merits as a basic allocative mechanism--which it never can or should be--but as one tool among many that can be utilized to effectuate desired ends. That the authors of the bill recognized this concept is reflected in the fact that the proposed law would allow for the condemnation of easements in situations where common-law doctrines might not find application.[67]

When viewed as one potential policy mechanism and not a panacea, the common-law approach as supported by the National Open Beaches Bill seems compatible with the Coastal Zone Management Act of 1972[68], which encourages the states to develop comprehensive programs of coastal resource management. When utilized at the state level, common-law techniques could be effective in implementing state management programs. At the federal level, the use of such tech-

67. H.R. 10394, sec. 204 (a) (3). For a discussion of easement acquisition and its relation to the shoreline situation, see Chapter 8 infra, at p. 147.

68. P.L. 92-583. See discussion infra, Chapter 11, at p. 207.

niques could also be tied in with the state programs, because the Act requires that "each federal agency conducting
or supporting activities directly affecting the Coastal Zone
shall conduct or support those activities in a manner which
is, to the maximum extent practicable, consistent with approved state management programs." It would seem
plausible that a beach access program carried out by the
Department of Justice under a Congressional open-beaches
mandate should be considered as within the purview of this
requirement. Thus, the common-law approach could be closely
coordinated with overall resource planning and management,
and this could go a long way in eliminating the difficulties
it tends to create when used in an ad hoc and fragmented fashion.

Whether or not the common-law approach is ever utilized
as envisioned above is a matter of pure speculation at this
point. For the present, court protection of public rights
should at least continue to provide a stimulus to legislative action and the necessary legitimization for a new perspective on coastal resource policy. With this in mind, we
will now turn to an examination of a number of other tools
that can be applied--this time through administrative ac-
tion--to the shoreline recreation problem.

---

69. Id., at sec. 307 (c) (1) .

Chapter 8

SHORELINE ACQUISITION FOR PUBLIC USE

1. Introduction

As we have seen, the dilemma posed by an increasing demand for and a decreasing supply of public recreational opportunities in the coastal shoreline has prompted a modicum of legislative and judicial activity. The aim has been to preserve existing public rights to use certain portions of the seashore--including some municipally-owned facilities--for recreational purposes. While these events represent an important beginning, the basic problem is far from solved. Opening up municipal beaches to the general public won't really make a dent in the potential demands, and it remains to be seen how far the legal doctrines discussed in Chapter 7 can be carried in upholding public claims in privately owned shorelands. And even if the common-law approach gains widespread acceptance, it is important to remember that it is only one of many techniques, and that posing the recreation issue solely in terms of public vs. private rights improperly places the burden of seeking a desirable resource distribution on the shoulders of the courts, who are ill-equipped and hesitant to deal with management issues of such great complexity. Striking a balance among private recreation, public recreation, conservation, and other uses of the seashore is a management problem and as such is the proper domain of the legislatures and their duly authorized agents. And since an expansion of public opportunities for shoreline recreation may require that tradeoffs be made with other socially-desirable objectives, it is essential that these tradeoffs be made in the context of a carefully thought-out management process.

The management of coastal resources must be dealt with within the framework of the allocative system outlined in Chapters 4 and 5, i.e. the combined mechanisms of the private market and collective (governmental) action. We have noted the economic fact of life that the private market, left alone, will under-produce certain desirable commodities under certain circumstances. Public beaches were cited as an example of such commodities - often referred to as "public goods" - the provision of which requires some collective interference with the workings of the market. But we have also noted that government activity is susceptible to certain forces which can inhibit effective allocative behavior. The costs and benefits that impinge on and determine the outcome of local decision-making are not the same costs and benefits that are felt on a region-wide basis. The real issue, then, is how to make an intelligent division of responsibility for allocative decision-making, not between government and the courts, but between the market and different levels of government.

As a first step in dealing with this issue it is important to examine the possible modes of government action, i.e. the tools of public policy available for resource allocation. In the remaining chapters of Part Two, we will deal primarily with this topic. The purpose is to outline how governmental bodies can compel, induce, or otherwise influence conduct regarding the use of land so as to expand public recreational oppportunities in the nation's shoreline. Included will be an examination of the power of government to uphold this component of the public interest through the expenditure of public funds and through police power regulation.

Before proceeding, we should note that the shoreline is essentially an open space, and public beaches or other coastal recreation areas are really public parks, so the applicable law is basically that which has been developed in the areas of open space and recreational park planning. However, coastal areas have an extra dimension in that they are part of the special environmental system that characterizes the land-sea interface. In the first place, the seashore has an element of physical uniqueness unmatched by other forms of urban parks and open spaces, and is particularly well suited to provide for scenic, aesthetic, historic, and other active and passive forms of public recreation not generally available in alternative locations. In the second place, the seashore has the element of ecological vulnerability arising from its integral relationship not only with the sea but also the land beyond the beach. Coastal recreation areas, then, are open spaces and parks, but they are also scarce, irreplaceable, and socially-valuable natural resources; in this sense, they can properly be considered the common property of all.

2. Acquisition Through Purchase and Condemnation

The most direct and frequently-used method of securing coastal areas for public recreational use is for a public agency to buy them, either through purchase or condemnation of the fee simple or an easement. It is firmly settled that

the federal government[1], the states[2], and municipalities[3] (when authorized by the state) have the constitutional
capacity to purchase or condemn land for park and recreational purposes. The power of eminent domain has repeatedly
been held to be an inherent attribute of the sovereign,
necessary for effective government operation.[4] This power
is limited by the United States Constitution's Fifth Amendment provision, "nor shall private property be taken for public use, without just compensation"[5], which also applies to
the states.[6] With regards the requirement that the taking
be for a public purpose, it has long been held that parks

---

1. Federal spending for recreational purposes cannot be
challenged in a taxpayer's suit, and therefore raises no
issue of constitutional legitimacy. Massachusetts v. Mellon
and Frothingham v. Mellon, 262 U.S. 447 (1923). The power
of the federal government to condemn land was first
established in Kohl v. United States, 91 U.S. 367 (1875).
The validity of federal condemnation programs can of course
be challenged in eminent domain proceedings.

2. See cases cited in Williams, Land Acquisition for Outdoor Recreation - Analysis of Selected Legal Problems, Outdoor Recreation Resources Review Commission Study Report No.
16, at 2-7 (1963). See also cases cited in Shoemaker v.
United States, 147 U.S. 282, 13 S.Ct. 361 (1839), and United
States v. Gettysburg Elec Ry., 160 U.S. 668, 16 S.Ct. 427
(1896).

3. Id.; See also Du Prev v. City of Marietta, 213 Ga. 403,
99 S.E. 2nd 156 (1957).

4. See Nichols, 1 Eminent Domain, s. 3.11 [1] (3d. ed.,
1950).

5. See Boom Co. v. Patterson, 98 U.S. 403 (1878).

6. Missouri Pac. Ry. v. Nebraska, 164 U.S. 403 (1896); By
this time, limitations of "public use" and "just
compensation" had been imposed on all state governments by
their constitutions or judicial rulings.

and other recreational facilities are legitimate objectives of public land use.[7] A companion limitation on eminent domain powers is the "necessity" test. While the courts have generally considered this a matter for the discretion of the legislature or their appointed administrative bodies[8], some have shown a willingness to consider how far in advance of immediate needs governments should condemn land.[9]

Since 1911, when the Weeks Act provided for the purchase of private lands to create national forests, the federal government has had its own park and forest programs. Today there exist a number of national parks bordering the coast[10] which provide passive recreational opportunities, while a series of national seashores[11] are available for

7. Village of Lloyd Harbor v. Town of Huntington, 4 N.Y. 2d 182, 149 N.E. 2d 851 (1958); Yosemite Park & Curry Co. v. Collins, 20 F.Supp. 1009 (N.D. Cal. 1937).

8. See Hagman, Urban Planning and Land Development Control Law, Chap. 14, n. 27 at 315 (1971).

9. The courts are divided on this issue. Compare Grand Rapids Board of Education v. Paczewski, 340 Mich. 265, 65 N.W. 2d 810 (1954). (Schools not needed for 30 years; acquisition of land for sites did not meet necessity test.) with Carlov Co. v. City of Miami, 62 So. 2d 897 (Fla.) cert. denied 346 U.S. 821 (1953) (Airport on inaccessible island clearly not needed for some time; city has both power and duty to provide for future needs and should not be limited to present exigencies.)

10. These include Acadia, Me. (1919); Olympic, Wash. (1938); Virgin Islands (1956).

11. Cape Hatteras National Seashore (1937), 16 U.S.C. s. 459 (1970); Cape Cod (1961), Point Reyes (1962), Padre Island (1962), Fire Island (1964), Assateague Island (1965), and Cape Lookout (1966). See 16 U.S.C. ss. 4596-4599 (1970). See also Chapter 3 infra, note 8, at p. 44.

active recreation. More significantly, the federal government has in the last decade or so provided grants to states,
counties, and cities for the acquisition of land for open
spaces, parks and related uses.[12] The most important of
these have been the Open-Space program[13], begun in 1961,
and the Land and Water Conservation Fund program of
1965.[14] The Open-Space program, administered by the Dept.
of Housing and Urban Development (HUD), authorizes matching
grants of up to 50 per cent to both states and local public
bodies in urban areas for the acquisition and limited development of, among other things, open space for park and re-

---

12. For an exhaustive description of federal grant-in-aid
programs for recreation, see U.S. Dept. of the Interior,
Bureau of Outdoor Recreation, Federal Outdoor Recreation
Programs and Recreation Related Environmental Programs
(1970). A most recent federal activity in this area is the
Surplus Property Program, which authorizes the Dept. of the
Interior to turn over surplus federal real estate to local-
ities for park purposes at very low prices or free of
charge. 40 U.S.C. s.485, 50 App. U.S.C. s. 1622. As of
June, 1972, 144 such properties had been made available for
recreational use, covering 20,000 acres in 39 states and
Puerto Rico, and mostly located in urban areas. Council on
Environmental Quality, Environmental Quality - Third
Annual Report (1972), at 138.

13. Title VII of Housing Act of 1961 (42 U.S.C. s. 1500),
amended by Title IV of Housing and Urban Development Act of
1970 (Pub. L. 91-609). This program has recently been combined with urban beautification and historic preservation
programs into a single comprehensive grant process, the A-95
Review Program.

14. 16 U.S.C. s. 460-(1) et seq.

creational purposes. Funds are appropriated by Congress each year ($100 million for fiscal 1973). Proposed projects must be in areas of "urban character" (this includes the suburbs), be important for carrying out an open-space program as part of a comprehensive plan for the entire urban area, and be permanently reserved for open space uses.[15] Under recent evaluation guidelines, HUD gives priority to Model Cities projects, low-and-moderate-income housing effects, and opportunities for employment of minority persons associated with the proposed project, while low ratings are given the preservation of scenic or ecologically significant areas.[16] While this might seem to afford beach acquisition a low priority, we should remember that the most pressing needs for water-oriented recreation opportunities are in urban areas where they can be made available to less mobile, lower income groups.

While the HUD Open-Space program serves many non-recreation objectives, the Land and Water Conservation Fund Program has as its major purpose the provision of outdoor recreational opportunities, especially in urbanized areas.[17] The Fund, administered by the Bureau of Outdoor Recreation, is financed through revenues from four sources (user fees at federal outdoor recreational areas; the sale of surplus federal real property; the federal motorboat fuel

---

15. Ells, "Massachusetts Open Space Law", Open Space and Recreation Program for Metropolitan Boston (1969), at 91-93.

16. Dawson, "Massachusetts Open Space Law Supplement-1972", 4 Open Space and Recreation Program for Metropolitan Boston (1969), at 36.

17. Ells, op. cit. note 15 supra, at 94.

tax; and off-shore oil and gas leases) and can be supple-
mented by advance appropriations by Congress, to be repaid
in later years. The minimum funding is $300 million an-
nually through 1989.[18] These monies can be used to finance
50 per cent of the cost of preparing and maintaining outdoor
recreation plans, and acquiring land and water areas for
outdoor recreation in accordance with a comprehensive statewide outdoor recreation plan. This program has been widely
recognized as the most far-reaching recreation measure yet
enacted by Congress.

At the state level, many large-scale open space programs
have been launched in the last decade. Such programs often
include state acquisition[19], grants-in-aid to local governments[20], and authorization and encouragement of land acquisition by municipalities for park and recreation pur-

---

18. Dawson, op. cit., note 16 supra, at 36.

19. See, e.g. Green Acres Land Acquisition Act of 1961, N.J.
Stat. Ann. ss.13: 8 A-1 et seq. (1968); Ore. Rev. Stat. s.
390.360 (1971) (Highway Commission can acquire ocean shoreland for recreational purposes); Chap. 742, Mass. Acts of
1970 (state acquisition of Boston Harbor Islands).
Frequently revenues are generated through bond issues. Over
the period 1962-1966, voters in twenty-four states approved
bond issues totalling $445 million for open-space purposes,
with an average plurality of 63 per cent. Whyte, The Last
Landscape, at 62-63 (1968).

20. Though the percentage varies from state to state, typically the states finance 25 per cent of the project cost.
Hence, local governments can multiply every dollar they put
up by three (and sometimes four) state and federal dollars.

poses.[21] At the local level, a few states have authorized
the creation of municipal conservation commissions, a relatively new and potentially effective tool with flexible
legal powers.[22] The commission is generally a town board
empowered with the conservation, promotion, and development
of the town's "natural resources", including wetlands, wood-
lands, open lands, birds, fish, soil, water, etc. The
commissions are usually authorized to make purchases based
on annual appropriations from the municipal government[23],
and are also directed to conduct resource planning and education activities.

3. Past Difficulties With the Acquisition Approach

The majority of planners see governmental acquisition programs as the most desirable means of providing public recreational facilites in the long run with minimal usurpation
of private rights.[24] While this is indeed true in princi-

---

21. These states include those most concerned with open
space and recreation programs, such as New York, New Jersey,
California, Maryland, Connecticut and Massachusetts. See
Eveleth, "An Appraisal of Techniques to Preserve Open
Space", 9 Villanova L. Rev..559 (1964) at 563, n. 21.

22. See Ells, op. cit., note 15 supra, at 15.

23. In New Jersey, all acquisition programs must be approved
by the local governing body. N.J. Stat. Ann. s. 40: 56A-1-3
(supp. 1969). In Massachusetts, town meeting approval is
necessary only when state or federal assistance is sought.
In 1960, the Massachusetts Self-Help Act (Act 517-1960) was
passed providing financial assistance to communities which
had established Conservation Commissions.

24. See e.g. Reis, "Policy and Planning for Recreational
Use of Inland Waters," 40 Temple L.Q. 155, at 182-183
(1967).

ple, there have been some very serious obstacles in practice. In Chapter 5, we noted that problems of cost and even
motivation (especially at the local level) have severely restricted the rate at which recreational shoreline can be acquired for public use. While acquisition programs proceed
at a snails pace, private development spreads rapidly with
little or no consideration being given to the extent to
which future public uses are being precluded. Another factor that has inhibited the effectiveness of acquisition programs is the narrow perspective some governmental agencies
have of the proper approach to recreation planning. Unfortunately, seashore areas seem to be viewed either as massive
public parks or as the exclusive domain of private owners.
This assumes implicitly that public use and private enjoyment are necessarily mutually exclusive, which they need not
always be. In the case of beaches, for example, the most
important geographic area for public use is the dry sand
area immediately adjacent to the water and extending to the
vegetation line. It is this portion of the beach that
should be the proximate object of government attention, and
it is important to note that its boundaries do not necessarily conform to those of the littoral owner's property.
In many cases, the sand areas is but a portion of the shorefront property, and the cost of its acquisition may be considerably less than the cost of the entire lot, as long as
multiple use can be accommodated in such a way as to preserve reasonable uses of the remaining land above the vegetation line. With proper planning, public use of the dry
sand portion of the seashore need not completely interfere
with private uses farther upland (especially since public
use is highly seasonal), and the aesthetic qualities of the
area need not be significantly disrupted in all cases.

A second mistake frequently made in the past and stemming from an all-or-nothing approach to shoreland acquisition is to forget about those areas for which acquisition and immediate intensive use by the public is not feasible. Too often, planners and government officials fail to treat the shoreline as open space which has the potential for future public use and therefore in need of conservation. As a result, beaches and bluff shores become lined with structures built almost right on the water's edge, while wetlands are dredged and filled. Not only does this obviate the possibility of future public acquisition, it is also dangerous for residential or commercial development from ecological and safety standpoints. The well-known open space planner, William H. Whyte, has emphasized this point in a number of his publications by saying that "the most unexploited opportunity for open space action is the conservation of land in private hands."[25]

4. Easements

Clearly, there is a need to apply more flexible legal techniques to the shoreline recreation problem than have been applied in the past. One such technique is the acquisition of an easement development or recreation rights or similar interests in property at less than fee simple.[26]

---

25. Whyte, Open Space Action, Outdoor Recreation Resources Review Commission Study Report No. 15, at 22 (1962).

26. See generally Note, "Techniques for Preserving Open Spaces", 75 Harv. L. Rev. 1622, at 1635 (1962); Comment, "Easements to Preserve Open Space Land", 1 Ecology L.Q. 728, at 731 (1972); Herring, ed.,Open Space and the Law, Institute of Governmental Studies, U. of California, Berkeley, at 41 (1965).

Under this approach, title to land remains in private hands
but is subject to constraints associated with the easement,
which can be either positive or negative depending on the
type of rights acquired. A positive easement secures for
the buyer the right to actually use the land in question
for specific purposes, whereas a negative easement limits
the uses to which the landowner himself may put the
land.[27] In either case, the compensation due the landowner
is the value of whatever property rights are relinquished,
as measured by the difference in the market price of the
land with and without the easement attached. This approach is thought to have several advantages over acquisition of the fee simple, the most significant of which is
the prospect of significantly lowering costs while still
achieving the same desired ends. The purchase price of an
easement is generally much lower than that of the fee
simple because only a portion of the total rights in
property are being acquired. And since an easement still
allows a landowner to use his land in any way not inconsistent with the terms of the easement, the land may continue
to be taxable (though at a somewhat reduced assessed
value). In contrast to the all-or-nothing approach inherent in fee simple acquisition, the easement approach
thus benefits greatly by treating property interests as a
"bundle of sticks" which can and should be divided when appropriate.

---

27. For an extensive discussion of negative easements, see
generally Whyte, Securing Open Space for Urban America:
Conservation Easements, Urban Land Institute Technical
Bulletin No. 36 (Dec. 1959).

Though not without its disadvantages,[28] purchase or condemnation of easements seems ideally-suited for the shoreline situation, and is clearly a prime candidate for future
consideration as a potentially effective policy tool. In
the first place, negative easements could provide a relatively inexpensive interim device for preserving coastal
open spaces for future acquisition for recreational purposes. A number of states have already enacted enabling
legislation providing for the purchase or condemnation of
conservation easements, development rights, or similar lesser interests in land for open space purposes.[29] There
seems no reason in principle why this technique could not
be applied along the coast,[30] where the development rights
to be conveyed to government would pertain to the erection
of buildings and other structures that either preclude future public use or damage the scenic or natural qualities
of the shorefront. Secondly, positive easements could be
utilized in some areas to acquire public recreation rights
in the shorefront portion of littoral properties, although
the cost might approach that of the fee simple if the degree of infringement on private uses for the property as a

---

28. For a recent discussion of the advantages and disadvantages of the easement approach, see Comments, "Easements to
Preserve Open Space Land", 1 Ecology L.Q. 728 (1971).

29. N.J. Stat. Ann. s. 13: 8A-6 (1961); N.Y. Conservation
Law, s. 1-0707 (c. 174 L. 1964); W. Va. Code Ann. ch. 20,
s. 2215; Cal. Gov't Code secs. 6950-54 (1966) and 51050-65
(1971).

30. Easement acquisition to achieve shoreline recreation
objectives has, in fact, been incorporated into the proposed National Open Beaches Bill, discussed supra, at p.126.

whole is great due to extensive public use. However, positive easements could be further divided into less than full recreation rights, and this might be useful, for example, in the case of a beach which is relatively narrow or is likely to be heavily populated. Whereas picnics, sunbathing, and other sedentary activities do cause large numbers to congregate and, therefore, difficulties, public strolling and beachcombing may be perfectly consistent with the full use and enjoyment of the private owner.

5. Concluding Remarks

In the long-run, government acquisition for public use is probably the most reliable method of increasing the supply of recreational opportunities in the coastal shoreline. If the cost of traditional acquisition programs is prohibitive, the purchase or condemnation of positive recreation easements in that portion of the shorefront immediately adjacent to the water may be a viable alternative. And if the time is not ripe for public use, conservation easements could be used to preserve suitable coastal areas as open space, not only because of their value for recreation but also because they are important ecologically and aesthetically.

There may, however, be circumstances in which any form of the acquisition approach may be infeasible or undesirable. In the first place, the costs of preserving large stretches of shoreline with fee simple or easement techniques may still be well beyond the means of government budgets. Secondly, it may be felt that the public should not have to pay to enjoy those portions of the nation's

shoreline traditionally open for public use, or at least
should not have to pay for the protection of this unique
natural environment when the costs should be borne by those
who threaten to damage it through indiscriminate use. The
common-law approach described in Chapter 7 dealt with the
former of these contentions, and it is now appropriate to
look at public policies involving non-compensable regulations to secure the public interest in the latter circum-
stance. In the following chapters, we will examine the extent to which the exercise of governmental police powers
and related legal devices can pick up where other tools
leave off.

Chapter 9

SHORELINE REGULATION I: THE POLICE POWER AND OPEN SPACE OBJECTIVES

1. Introduction

The discussions in Chapters 7 and 8 indicate that, in the long run, significant increases in public recreation opportunities in the coastal shoreline can be effected in a variety of ways (e.g. purchase or condemnation, easement acquisition, affirmation of pre-existing public rights, etc.) But if beaches and other prime recreational shorelands currently unavailable for public use are to be "reclaimed" with the help of such techniques, they should be treated in the interim as open spaces so as to preserve those portions of the shore most appropriate for public use. To see how land-use regulation might be applied to the shoreline recreation situation, it is necessary to outline the source of the police power and the scope of its exercise in connection with the preservation of open spaces. The purpose of this chapter is to examine the constitutional limitations of the regulatory power of state government and the factors considered by the courts in determining the validity of open space regulations. This will set the stage for the discussions in Chapter 10 of the specific tools that can be utilized to meet open space objectives in seashore areas.

The police power is essentially the authority of state government to regulate the activities of individuals in order to foster public health, safety, morals, and the general welfare.[1] It is, in effect, the right of the states to

---

1. See Lawson v. Steele, 152 U.S. 133 at 136-137 (1894); In Chicago B.&Q. Ry v. Illinois ex rel Drainage Comm'rs, 200 U.S. 561, at 592-594 (1906), the Court held that the police power "embraces regulation designed to promote the public convenience or the general prosperity."

legislate in the public interest and represents an immense
and indefinable mass of legislative authority to promote the
public welfare by "restraining and regulating the use of
liberty and property."[2] This authority does not flow from
constitutional sources but from the courts, who have affirmed the police power as integral to the concept of state
government. Ever since the landmark Supreme Court decisions
of the 1920's upholding the constitutionality of zoning, the
police power has been applied in numerous forms by the
several states or their political subdivisions to control
land-use for the health, safety, morals, and general welfare
of the community. Over this period, the concept of what
serves the general welfare has continually expanded. To the
historical rationales of controlling density[3] and preserving
property values[4] have been added aesthetic[5], cultural-histo-

---

2. Freund, The Police Power, at 23 (1904).

3. The most frequently cited traditional goals of zoning are
to lessen street congestion; secure safety from fire, panic,
and other dangers; provide adequate light and air; prevent
overcrowding of land; avoid undue concentration of population; and facilitate adequate provision of transport,
water, sewerage, schools, parks, and other public requirements. See U.S. Dept. of Commerce. A Standard State Zoning
Enabling Act (1926).

4. While the preservation of property values was the most
important political motivation for the widespread acceptance
of zoning and other land-use controls, it was not explicitly
recognized by the courts until some time later. See, e.g.
Rockhill v. Chesterfield Township, 23 N.J. 117, 128 A.2d 473
(1956).

5. See People v. Stover, 12 N.Y. 2d 462, 191 N.E. 2d 272
(1963); State v. Diamond Motors, Inc., 50 Hawaii 33, 429 P.
2d 825 (1967); see also cases cited in Broesche, "Land Use
Regulation for the Protection of Public Parks and Recreational Areas", 45 Texas Law Review 96, at 108-110 (1966).

ric[6], scenic[7], architectural[8] and other "amenity"[9] objectives, as well as the encouragement of the most appropriate
use of land within a community.[10] In the frequently-cited
case of <u>Berman v. Parker</u>, Justice Douglas offered the following perspective on the public welfare:

> Public safety, public health, morality,
> peace and quiet, law and order -- these
> are some of the more conspicuous examples
> of the traditional application of the po-
> lice power to municipal affairs. Yet
> they merely illustrate the scope of the
> power and do not delimit it... The con-
> cept of the public welfare is broad and
> inclusive. The values it represents are
> spiritual as well as physical, aesthetic
> as well as monetary. It is within the
> power of the legislature to determine
> that the community should be beautiful as
> well as healthy, spacious as well as
> clean, well-balanced as well as carefully
> controlled.[11]

---

6. The Vieux Carre Ordinance in New Orleans is the best
known ordinance designed to preserve a cultural-historic
area. See La. Const. Art. 14, s. 22A.

7. See Scenic Hudson Preservation Conference v. Federal
Power Commission, 354 F. 2d 608 (2d. Cir. 1965), <u>cert.
denied</u>, 384 U.S. 941 (1966).

8. See State ex rel Saveland Park Holding Corp. v. Wieland,
269 Wis. 262, 69 N.W. 2d 217 (1955).

9. Other amenities that have been held to be within the
general welfare include public enjoyment, a right to be free
from unwelcome obstructions, preservation of mental
well-being, comfort, and convenience. See cases cited in
Broesche, op. cit., note 5 <u>supra</u>, at 103.

10. See Lionhead Lake, Inc. v. Township of Wayne, 10 N.J.
165, 89 A.2d 693 (1952).

11. 348 U.S. 26, 75 Sup.Ct. 98 (1954).

Based on judicial language of this sort and the criteria
developed for determining the validity of police power
measures in the aforementioned areas, a number of commentators have concluded that land-use regulation for the protection of open spaces[12] as well as public parks and recreational areas[13] can readily be supported. A number of
communities have, in fact, employed various forms of open
space controls, including flood plain[14], agricultural[15],
and recreational zones.[16] The common characteristic of all
such controls is that they are designed to prevent or
seriously restrict building construction in particular
areas.[17] The range of objectives sought includes preservation of prime natural areas such as forests or wetlands;
prevention of flood losses; protection of scenic or his-

12. See Comment, "Techniques for Preserving Open Spaces", 75
Harv. L. Rev. 1622, at 1623 (1962).

13. See Broesche, op. cit., note 5 supra, at 110.

14. See Dunham, "Flood Control via the Police Power", 107 U.
Pa. L. Rev. 1098 (1958).

15. See Ott, The Need, Constitutionality and Limitation of
Agricultural Zoning, Fresno, California. (1957).

16. This will be discussed in full infra, at p. 172.

17. In a recent article on open space law, Kusler uses the
term "open space zoning" to refer to the whole range of
special wetland, flood plain, lakeshore, coastal, scenic
preservation, and other protection districts, in addition to
the more conventional techniques of building setbacks, official mapping, and park land dedication requirements in subdivision regulations. See Kusler, "Open Space Zoning: Valid
Regulation or Invalid Taking", 57 Minn. L. Rev. 1, at 5,
n.5.

toric areas; control of urban sprawl;   and   protection   of
park   and   recreation   areas.[18]In pursuing these and   other
open space   objectives,   there   is   always the clear possibility that government action will result in a substantial
infringement on private property rights, and it behooves us
to examine the approach that courts have taken in resolving
the conflicts that are likely to ensue.[19]

2. Constitutional Limitation of Regulatory Power

There is general agreement that   the   scope   of the police
power has and will continue to expand   as   the problems of
industrial   society   become more complex, and as government
is increasingly called upon to regulate private conduct as
a means of achieving   desired   social objectives. But this
trend must be balanced against   the   claims of private persons to be protected against the unjustifiable sacrifice of
their individual   rights.   The bulwark for these claims is
the U.S. Constitution, whose   provisions   as interpreted by
the   courts   limit   the scope of   the   police   power.   The
Fourteenth   Amendment   to the U.S. Constitution states that
"nor   shall   any state deprive any person of life, liberty,
or property, without   due   process   of   law;   nor   deny any
person within its jurisdiction the equal   protection of the
laws." This "due process" doctrine establishes a baseline
standard of   fairness and requires that "the law shall not

18. Id. at 5, n.6.

19. In the remainder of the present chapter, discussion will
be limited to general constitutional considerations. In
Chapter 10, these considerations will be applied to the
specific regulatory tools that are relevant to the
shorelands situation.

be unreasonable, arbitrary or capricious, and that the
means selected shall have a real and substantial relation
to the object sought to be attained."[20] A companion requirement which has been incorporated[21] into the Fourteenth
Amendment states that "nor shall private property be taken
for public use, without just compensation."[22]

In a series of cases beginning in 1926, the Supreme
Court established broad guidelines with respect to the
constitutionality of regulatory measures designed to control the use of land. In Euclid v. Ambler[23], the first
Supreme Court test of zoning, the court spoke to the issues
of reasonableness and the relation of regulatory measures
to the goal desired:

> The ordinance now under review, and all
> similar laws and regulations, must find
> their justification in some aspect of
> the police power, asserted for the pub-
> lic welfare. The. line which in this
> field separates the legitimate from the
> illegitimate assumptions of power is not
> capable of precise delimitation.   It

---

20. Nebbia v. New York, 291 U.S. 502, at 525 (1934).

21. Chicago B. & Q. R.R. v. Chicago, 166 U.S. 226, 235-41
(1897).

22. U.S. Const. amend. V. We should note that this is never
an absolute prohibition in relation to the police power, as
distinguished from the power of eminent domain. The very
essence of the police power is that some individual rights
in property can be deprived in behalf of the general
welfare, as long as the regulatory method is proper and its
exercise is reasonable within the meaning of due process.
See, e.g. Commonwealth v. Alger, 61 Mass. (7 Cush.) 53, at
84-86 (1851).

23. 272 U.S. 365, 47 Sup. Ct. 114 (1926).

varies with the circumstances....If the
validity of the legislative classification for zoning purposes be fairly debatable, the legislative judgement must
be allowed to control.

If these reasons, thus summarized, do
not demonstrate the wisdom or sound
policy in all respects of those restrictions which we have indicated as pertinent to the inquiry, at least, the
reasons are sufficiently cogent to preclude us from saying, as must be said
before the ordinance can be declared unconstitutional, that such provisions are
clearly arbitrary and unreasonable,
having no substantial relation to the
public health, safety, morals or general
welfare.[24]

In <u>Nectow v. City of Cambridge,</u>[25] the second leading
Supreme Court zoning case, the court demonstrated its
willingness to consider the impact of zoning restrictions
on property uses as well as on the public health, safety,
and welfare.[26] Finally, in <u>Zahv v. Board of Public</u>

---

24. Id.

25. 277 U.S. 183, 48 Sup. Ct. 447 (1928).

26.   "that the invasion of the property of
         plaintiff in error was serious and highly
         injurious is clearly established; and,
         since a necessary basis for the support
         of that invasion is wanting, the action
         of the zoning authorities comes within
         the ban of the Fourteenth Amendment and
         cannot be sustained."

Id.

Works,[27] the court reaffirmed the doctrines ennunciated in Euclid and Nectow, and then retired from consideration of zoning issues. This left the state courts with three general factors[28] to consider when determining whether a given regulatory measure constitutes a taking without due process: (1) the objectives or basic philosophy of the regulation; (2) the reasonableness of the regulations: and (3), the extent of the impact on private interests.

As practice developed at both federal and state levels, it became clear that the first two of these factors would be relatively straightforward to evaluate, and courts have developed basic approaches to each. With regard to overall objectives, the scrutiny of regulatory measures is tempered by a strong deference in favor of the legislative authority of the states to make flexible use of the police power in response to changing economic and social condi-tions.[29] With regard to the reasonableness of specific

---

27. 247 U.S. 325. The court affirmed the settled rule that "it will not substitute its judgement for that of the leg-islative body charged with primary duty and responsibility for determining the question." The court also considered the detrimental effect on property value that the regu-lation in question engendered, and found no clearly unreasonable or arbitrary activity by the regulatory authority.

28. For an extensive discussion of these three factors, see Anderson, "A Comment on the Fine Line Between 'Regulation' and 'Taking'", The New Zoning: Legal Administrative, and Economic Concepts and Techniques, (Marcus and Groves ed., 1970).

29. See Johnson, "Constitutional Law and Community Planning", 20 Law & Contemporary Problems 199 (1955); West Coast Hotel Co. v. Parrish, 300 U.S. 379 (1937).

provisions, on the other hand, the courts have not hesi-
tated to examine administrative actions, especially in circumstances which seem threatening to the doctrine that
equally-situated property owners should be equally
treated.[30] However, the evolution of judicial approaches
to the question of what is taking without due process has
not been so clear cut in situations where neither the objectives nor the reasonableness of regulations is in doubt.
In such cases, any growth in the concept of valid exercise
of the police power inevitably forces a reevaluation of
situations that have traditionally been viewed as an invalid taking. This has created a "gray area, or twilight
zone of constitutionality"[31] within which lies the distinction between justifiable regulation and confiscation. And
since open space regulations are generally thought to be
well within the scope of the police power, it becomes
important to investigate the determinants of constitutionality with regards this 'taking' issue in open space
cases.

3. Regulation or Confiscation?

The first factor important in the determination of whether
a regulation is really a taking is the existence of a
property right. It is often said that property is a

---

30. The case law on "spot" zoning is illustrative of this
point. See e.g. Kuehne v. Town Council of East Hartford,
136 Conn. 452, 72 A. 2d 474 (1950).

31. Broesche, op. cit. note 5 supra, at 100.

"bundle of sticks", a collection of present, future, and intangible[32] interests that are capable of transfer between private owners.[33] If no property rights exist[34], there can be no taking, by definition. Property is generally taken by the acquisition of title to an interest in property, but taking can also constitute physical invasion or use, or a substantial interference by government which deprives a property owner of all or most of the beneficial use.[35]

In the absence of any of the above factors, the question of what is a taking without due process has never been settled with any authority by the courts. One criteria that had been espoused by a number of legal commentators is that a regulation is a taking if it is designed to benefit the public rather than to prevent harm. Strangely enough, this apparently straightforward concept has managed to

---

32. These include light, air, accessibility, and other intangible rights "incidental to the ownership of land itself". See Nicols, 2 The Law of Eminent Domain, secs. 6.3-6.38, 6.44 (1963).

33. This concept of "transferability", though appearing in different forms, is common to all definitions of property for which the confiscation question applies. For example, Sax conceives of property as a multitude of existing interests, or "economic values defined by a process of competition", not inconsistent with the interests of other property owners. Sax, "Taking and the Police Power", 74 Yale L. J. 36, at 61 (1964).

34. There is no property right to maintain a nuisance, and no property right in the public domain. See Hagman, Urban Planning and Land Development Control Law, s. 180, at 325 (1971).

35. Id., s. 179, at 320.

elude precise definition, and its application to factual
situations has failed to yield consistently satisfactory
results. An early statement of the doctrine was formulated
by Freund, who asserted that "the state takes property by
eminent domain because it is useful to the public, and
under the police power because it is harmful."[36] In 1958,
Dunham attempted to establish the legitimacy of this test
through empirical observation, and concluded the regulation
is generally upheld when it prevents harmful externalities
(uncompensated costs on other parties) and not when a
"good" is conferred on the public.[37] Nevertheless, the test
as stated is often difficult to apply in subtle situations.[38] Probably the most rigorous statement of the general criteria was developed in 1964 by Sax, who made a dis-

---

36. Freund, The Police Power, Public Policy and Constitutional Rights, s. 511, at 546-547 (1904).

37. In reviewing a large number of cases, Dunham concluded:

> "...Where the legislation was upheld,
> the purpose and effect of the
> legislation was to allocate to a land
> use the costs which, but for the
> legislation, the activity would impose
> on other owners without compensation.
> In each instance where the legislation
> was struck down, the purpose and effect
> of the legislation was to compel one or
> more particular owners to furnish
> without compensation a benefit wanted by
> the public."

Dunham, "A Legal and Economic Basis for City Planning", 58
Colum.L.Rev. at 669 (1958).

38. Hagman cites the example of flight plane zoning and
asks if such regulations are designed to prevent buildings
above the flight plane which could harm passengers in
airplanes, or to acquire for the public good a highway in
the sky. Hagman, op.cit., note 34, supra, at 326.

tinction between the two different types of private economic loss resulting from government activity, corresponding
to two different roles played by government in competitive
processes. His test for the validity of a regulation
followed from this distinction:

> ... when economic loss is incurred as a
> result of government enhancement of its
> resource position in its enterprise ca-
> pacity, the compensation is constitu-
> tionally required; it is that result
> which is to be characterized as a
> taking. But losses, however severe,
> incurred as a consequence of government
> acting in its arbitral capacity are to
> be viewed as a noncompensable exercise
> of the police power.[39]

While this construction of the taking test embodies important insights regarding the relationship of law to the
role government plays in the economic system, it does not
escape the inherent drawbacks of the benefit-compelling vs.
harm-preventing concept   to   which it is closely related.[40] It is true that when government acts in its enterprise capacity, it generally seeks to provide the public
with a beneficial good or service; and, when it acts in its
arbitral capacity, it generally seeks to prevent a hazard
to the general welfare.   But regardless of the precision
with which the distinction is drawn, there still exist

---

39. Sax, op. cit., note 33 supra, at 62-65.

40. Sax acknowledged this difficulty in a subsequent major
article, "Takings, Private Property, and Public Rights", 81
Yale L.J. 149 (1971), in which he disowned the view that
whenever government can be said to acquire resources on its
own account, compensation must be paid.   This will be discussed further infra, at p. 214.

situations   where   a   regulation   may   be   said with equal
truth   to   confer benefits on the public or to save it from
harm.   One   commentator   has   illustrated this point   with
reference to the development of lands that serve as natural
flood storage areas:

> ... while the filling of natural storage
> areas   may   increase   flood   heights   on
> other lands and therefore result in cer-
> tain nuisance-like   effects, regulations
> which   prevent such filling require   one
> owner to   maintain his land as a storage
> area   to   benefit other owners   and   the
> public.[41]

As a general rule, whenever it is the public that is the
recipient of harmful   side   effects   from   certain property
uses, it is artificial   to   attempt   to   classify   remedial
regulations as   "harm-preventing"   or "benefit-compelling",
since the harm that is prevented is identical to the benefit   that   is   conferred,   and   the   terms   become   inter-
changeable.[42]   In trying to deal with such situations, many
courts   have begun to validate regulations   that   could   be
characterized   as seeking a benefit for the community.[43]   In

---

41. Kusler, op. cit., note 17 supra, at 18.

42. Other frequently cited examples of this phenomenon are
setback regulations for traffic safety; airport zoning; and
even comprehensive   zoning in general.   See Institute   for
Governmental Studies,   Univ. of California, Berkeley, Open
Space and the Law, at 10 (Herring, ed., 1965).

43. A somewhat typical   response   on   the part of the judiciary has been to expand the concept of what is a harm that
can properly be restricted to the point   where   it   encompasses some of   what   were   previously considered benefits.
This is part of the general expansion of the concept of the
"public welfare" as a permissible objective of governmental
regulation. See Hagman, "Planning Legislation: 1963", 30
J. Am. Inst. Planners 247, at 251, 254 n. 23 (1964).

the absence of a reliable, simplified test for determining whether or not a 'taking' exists, the courts have resorted to a balancing process which weighs the societal benefit of a particular regulation against the impact on individual ownership of land.[44] An early indication of judicial reliance on this process was the decision in <u>Pennsylvania Coal Co. v. Mahon</u>,[45] where the Supreme Court found unconstitutional a statute which prohibited mining of coal in such a way as to cause the settling of nearby residences into the ground. In finding no public interest "sufficient to warrant so extensive a destruction of the defendant's constitutionally protected rights,"[46] Holmes is thought to have forecast the balancing technique which has characterized Supreme Court as well as state court handling of due process litigation.[47] What then, are the factors that enter into this balancing process and how do they apply to the open space situation?

---

44. "The decisions suggest that the process is one of balancing the public good which the regulation is intended to secure against the deprivation of use value suffered by the owner of the restricted land." Anderson, op. cit. note 28 <u>supra</u>, at 81. See also Kusler, op. cit. note 17 <u>supra</u>, at <u>5</u>; Anderson, 1 <u>The American Law of Zoning</u>, s. 2.19 at 80-81 (1968).

45. 260 U.S. 393, 435 Sup. Ct. 158 (1922).

46. "The general rule at least is that while property may be regulated to a certain extent, if regulation goes too far, it will be recognized as a taking." Id., at 415.

47. See Anderson, op.cit. note 28 <u>supra</u>, at 69.

4. Factors in Judicial Review of Open Space Regulations

In a recent article, Jon A. Kusler, a leading scholar in
the field of open space law, has divided the factors
relevant to the question of taking in open space regulation
cases into two categories: (1) those related to public
harm, including protection of public safety, prevention of
nuisances, and promotion of aesthetics; and (2), those
involving infringement on private property (including
physical invasion, vested rights over the regulation
period, diminuition of value, and denial of all reasonable
use.)[48] Since most of Kusler's observations are pertinent
to the topic of interest in this book, it is useful to
review briefly his discussion of each of the above factors.

4.1 Protection of Public Safety
The degree of destruction
of private property allowed by the courts has always been a
function of the priority of social objectives regulations
are designed to serve, and Kusler points out that public
health and safety have always enjoyed a "special presumption of constitutionality."[49] Since controls that are
reasonably related to these goals are almost invariably
sustained, "specific provisions in open space regulations
which prohibit or severely restrict uses posing threats to
public safety are likely to be upheld."[50]

4.2 Prevention of Nuisances
Regulations designed to pre-
vent nuisances that have adverse effects on the public wel-

---

48. Kusler, op. cit., note 17 supra, at 20 et seq.

49. Id. at 21.

50. Id. at 22.

fare are generally sustained. Even when substantial
financial losses are incurred by individual property
owners,[51] it is thought that such individuals enjoy a
reciprocal benefit in that the restrictions prohibit others
from generating similar nuisances. But, as Kusler asserts,
open space regulations are unlike other land use controls
which provide reciprocal benefits since they are generally
more restrictive and benefit the regulated owners little if
at all.[52] In addition, open space regulations are
generally not created explicitly to prevent nuisances;
their purposes are clearly to provide certain benefits to
the public. Kusler concludes that the various theories of
nuisance prevention "do not lend support to open space
zoning."[53]

4.3 Promotion of Aesthetics If one views the promotion of
aesthetic as the prevention of visual nuisances, it might
be plausible to relate this class of open space objectives
to traditional nuisance doctrines. However, many courts
have been reluctant to sanction such a view because of the
subjective nature of what is aesthetically pleasing and
because amenity values have generally been accorded lower
priority relative to more conventional notions of public
health and safety.[54]

---

51. See e.g. Hadacheck v. Los Angeles, 239 U.S. 394 (1915).

52. Kusler, op. cit. note 17 supra, at 7.

53. Id. at 28.

54. Id. at 29.

4.4 Physical Invasion The physical invasion of land by
government violates the territorial sovereignty of private
property, and it is almost universally held that this constitutes a taking.[55] Thus, "governmental attempts to permit
the public use of private lands for parks, parking lots,
golf courses and other areas, without compensating the
landowner are likely to fail as unconstitutional takings."[56]

4.5 Vested Rights and the Regulation Period   The   courts
have generally accorded greater weight to "vested" private
property rights in existing uses than to future uses,[57] but
restrictions on future developments depend heavily on duration.   Thus, "while interim regulations which   freeze
development for several years have been sustained, regulations which prohibit development of whole properties for
long or indefinite periods have with little exception been
disapproved."[58]

4.6 Diminuition of Value The diminuition in value test was
originally put forth by Holmes in Pennsylvania Coal Co. v.
Mahon,[59] and attention to the extent of a land-owners

---

55. Michelman, "Property, Utility and Fairness: Comments
on the Ethical Foundations of 'Just Compensation' Law", 80
Harvard L. Rev. 1165, 1184 (1967).

56. Kusler, op. cit. note 17 supra, at 32. But see Chapter
10 infra, at p.175.

57. See cases cited, Id., at 32 n. 108.

58. Id. at 32-33.

59. 260 U.S. 393, at 413 (1922). "When diminution reaches
a certain magnitude, in most if not all cases there must be
an exercise of eminent domain and compensation to sustain
·the act."

economic deprivation is given in almost every case involving the constitutionality of a land-use regulation.[60] However, the diminuition test by itself has not provided a consistently satisfactory criteria for determining whether a taking has occurred.[61] Kusler suggests that it is the effect of the diminuition in value on the reasonable use of land, and not the amount, that seems to be the crucial factor.[62]

4.7 Denial of All Reasonable Use   While diminuition in value is not necessarily grounds for unconstitutionality, a regulation which deprives a land-owner of all "reasonable", "beneficial", or "practical" use of his property generally effects an unconstitutional taking.[63] All of these adjectives refer in most cases to profitable uses rather than any possible use, but do not imply that a land-owner must be allowed the most beneficial use of his land.[64] After reviewing a number of leading cases on the issue, Kusler as-

---

60. Anderson, op. cit. note 28 supra, at 71.

61. Anderson examined approximately fifty cases in which courts specifically mentioned the diminuition in value suffered by a landowner as a result of zoning ordinances. He found that half were upheld and the other half struck down, suggesting that such loss is not a single or decisive factor where the loss is short of confiscation. See Anderson, 1 American Law of Zoning, s. 2.23 (1968); Kusler found that in fifty cases where regulations were found invalid, the weighted mean reduction in value was 73 per cent. In fifty cases validating regulations, the weighted mean reduction was 60 per cent. See Kusler, op. cit. note 17 supra, at 33

62. Kusler, op. cit. note 17 supra, at 34.

63. See cases cited Id., at 35, n. 123.

64. Id. at 36.

serts that open space regulation limiting lands to certain
public activities may enable economic uses for rural areas
with low land values, but it "is doubtful that such uses
allow an economic return for recreational lands located
along lakes and rivers where property values and taxes are
usually high."[65] In addition, "regulations affecting
swamps, steep slopes, erosion areas and flood hazard areas
may be invalidated if the permitted uses are not sufficiently remunerative to allow economic reclamation of the
lands."[66]

5. Concluding Remarks

The most recent analysis of current case law involving the
taking issue in land-use situations cites regulations for
preservation of open spaces (including flood prone areas,
wetlands and estuarine zones, and beach lands) as a major
category of controls which often generates litigation based
on taking claims.[67] While open space regulations have a
basis in logic and are increasingly looked upon favorably by
many courts as part of an expanded concept of the public
welfare, they clearly run the risk of confrontation with
well-established judicial precedents on both sides of the
balancing test. First, with regards the infringement of
private interests, areas placed in open space zones are often subject to physical restrictions that limit profitable
uses. When open space regulations severely restrict con-

---

65. Id. at 41.

66. Id. at 63.

67. For an extensive discussion of each element in this category, see Bosselman, Callies, and Banta, The Taking Issue,
Washington, D.C. (1973), at 139 et seq. (Chapter 9).

struction of all or most buildings, they reduce land values to a much greater extent than convential zoning. Second, with regards the potential benefit to society, there is far less than universal support of police power measures to achieve specialized open space objectives, which cannot always be related to traditionally-accepted goals of public health and safety. While there is evidence that this situation is changing rapidly, until recently open space preservation has been accorded only "second-class" status as a member of the family of legitimate police power objectives.[68]

The uncertain constitutional ground upon which open space controls are likely to stand has led Kusler to the following conclusions:

> Regulatory approaches are less likely subject to constitutional attack if they simutaneously permit private landowners some economic uses for their lands and yet considerably restrict uses in order to achieve public objectives. The key to constitutionality appears to be in this balance.[69]

With this philosophy in mind, we can now turn to an examination of the specific regulatory techniques that might be applied to preserving shore areas for open-space use. This is the topic in Chapter 10.

---

68. Id., at 195 et seq. But see the discussion and references infra, at p. 201.

69. Kusler, op. cit. note 17 supra, at 65.

SHORELINE REGULATION II: LAND-USE CONTROLS FOR
SEASHORE PRESERVATION

1. Introduction

The purpose of this chapter is to examine some specific regulatory tools that might be applied in the shoreline recreation situation; and to evaluate these tools within the context of the constitutional factors discussed in Chapter 9,
i.e. the tradeoff between the extent of infringement on private interests and the degree of protection or promotion of
the public welfare. Since this balancing process has never
been governed by a definable judicial calculus, courts "have
tended to limit the scope of their decisions to the issues
and circumstances before them, declaring that it is not in
the nature of things that any definitive list of the police
power's applications can be drawn up."[1] Thus, it is important to focus on the factual characteristics of each class
of cases in order to discuss which elements or factors are
likely to be determinative of the validity of regulatory
measures when applied to shore recreation situations.

2. Exclusive Use Zoning

The surest method of preserving a shore area for recreational use would be to create a special zoning district which
allows only recreation and related open-space uses. While
these may be the most appropriate uses of the land in question and be consistent with broad local and regional needs,
the regulation will almost certainly be declared invalid if

---

1. Netherton, "Implementation of Land Use Policy: Police
Power vs. Eminent Domain," 3 Land & Water L. Rev. 33, at 38
(1968).

it deprives private shore owners of any beneficial use. A
long line of leading cases have verified that the degree of
restriction is the controlling factor. In Arvene Bay Construction Co. v. Thatcher[2], the court declared that a zoning
ordinance must leave the owner some opportunity to derive
some reasonable use and benefit from his property. In City
of Plainfield v. Borough of Middlesex[3], a zoning ordinance
designed to discourage prospective buyers of a particular
tract was struck down by the courts as too restrictive, even
though the land was appropriate for the zoned purposes. In
Morris County Land Improvement Co. v. Township of Parsippany-Troy Hills[4], the court struck down as too restrictive a
zoning ordinance which attempted to preserve certain marsh
areas in their natural state as watershed basins and wildlife sanctuaries. In Forde v. Miami Beach[5], an ordinance
which had the effect of permitting only uneconomical development (single family residences in a beach area of high
reclamation cost) was disallowed. These and a host of other
cases all indicate that an ordinance which prohibits all
uses except certain recreational and conservational activities well may be invalidated where there is a great diminution in the value of the land and/or when none of the per-

---

2. 278 N.Y. 222, 15 N.E. 2d 587 (1938).

3. 69 N.J. Super. 136, 173 A. 2d 785 (1961). The borough
had unsuccessfully tried to buy the land for school and park
purposes, and resorted to the police power to attempt to
achieve the same objectives.

4. 40 N.J. 539, 193 A. 2d 232 (1963).

5. 146 Fla. 676, 1 So. 2d 642 (1941).

mitted uses can yield a reasonable economic return.[6]

Where regulations permit at least some reasonable degree of use, the courts have been divided and the decisions have varied with the circumstances. However, certain classes of objectives seem to be accorded greater priority than others. For example, we noted in the previous Chapter that ordinances are frequently upheld when they can be related to the traditionally-accepted goal of public safety. The preservation of certain unique natural areas seems also to enjoy special protection in certain jurisdictions. In Walker v. Board of County Commissioners,[7] for example, an oil company's shorefront property was zoned agricultural/residential, uses of much less value than the refinery the company had intended to build. Nevertheless, the court held that the ordinance did not deprive the company of all beneficial use, and attached great significance to the stated intent of the ordinance to preserve the natural characteristics of the Chesapeake Bay area. Such cases provide a sharp contrast to the leading case of Vernon Park Realty Co. v. City of Mount Vernon,[8] where a parcel in the middle of a highly developed business district was zoned for parking only. The property was clearly profitable for parking (although more valuable for other commercial uses) and the city argued that any other use would have adverse effects on traffic congestion in an already saturated area. Nevertheless, the court invalidated the ordinance, stating that the exercise of such

6. See Chapter 9 infra, at p. 171. But see infra, note 10, at p. 175.

7. 208 Md. 72, 116 A. 2d 393 (1955).

8. 307 N.Y. 493, 121 N.E. 2d 517 (1954).

power is arbitrary or unreasonable "whenever [it] precludes the use of the property for any purpose for which it is adapted."[9]

From the foregoing discussion, it seems clear that three factors are highly determinative of the validity of exclusive use zones: first, the appropriateness of the land for the uses allowed; second, the degree of restriction of reasonable uses; and third, the extent of the public necessity perceived by the courts.[10] The question now is, what is the validity of exclusive recreation or open space zones in shore areas? To answer this, we can look at two relevant types of regulations: (1) beach recreation zoning, and (2) flood plain zoning.

2.1 Beach Recreation Zoning   Fortunately, one of the leading cases on zoning in general is also a beach recreation case: McCarthy v. City of Manhattan Beach.[11] In McCarthy, the California Supreme Court sustained a zoning ordinance which restricted ocean-front property to beach recreation

---

9. 307 N.Y. 493, 121 N.E. 2d 517 (1954). It might be argued that this is a misrepresentation of the rule that an ordinance is unconstitutional only when it "so restricts the use of property that it cannot be used for any reasonable purpose." Arvene Bay Constr. Co. v. Thatcher, 278 N.Y. 222 (1938). In fact, this point was the foundation for the dissenting opinion in Vernon Park.

10. A noted commentator has observed that "a very high degree of diminution of value of property through restriction of allowable uses may be tolerated if the public necessity is great." Waite, "The Dilemma of Water Recreation and a Suggested Solution", 1958 Wisconsin L. Rev. 542, at 608.

11. Cal. 2d 879, 264 P. 2d 932 (1953); cert. denied 348 U.S. 817 (1954).

purposes, allowing only the operation of recreational facilities for an admission fee. To understand the full significance of this holding, it is useful to examine the facts
in some detail.

The plaintiffs owned three-fifths of a mile of sandy
beach, varying in width from 174 to 186 feet, bordered to
the west by the Pacific Ocean and to the east by a state
park. Since 1900, the land in question had been used continually by the public for beach recreational purposes, and
in 1924 the city brought an action claiming that the land
had been dedicated to public use. In 1938, having failed to
establish the land in public ownership, the city co-operated
with the plaintiffs in a number of unsuccessful attempts to
persuade the county or the state to purchase the land. In
1940, the plaintiffs attempted to erect and maintain a wire
fence enclosing the beach, with the intent of charging admission fees. Claiming no value for residential subdivision, they then requested that the property be rezoned under
a 1929 ordinance from single-family residential to commercial. This was denied, and the plan to fence off the beach
was abandoned apparently because the public had continually
destroyed parts of the fence. Then, in 1941, the city
adopted a comprehensive zoning ordinance which placed the
plaintiff's property in a "beach recreation district." The
only structures allowed were lifeguard towers, open smooth
wire fences, and small signs, and the owner was permitted to
charge admission fees. From 1941 until 1950, the plaintiffs
made no use of their property as permitted under the zoning
ordinance, and in 1950 they applied for a zoning reclassifi-
cation back to single-family residential. (This was pro-

bably motivated by a desire to increase the "fair compensation" value of the property, since condemnation proceedings had been initiated at the state level but had not yet come to trial by 1950.) This was denied, and the plaintiffs attacked the ordinance on the ground that it was an unreasonable taking of property and that it was passed in bad faith to depress their property value to enable acquisition at a lower price.

In the words of one commentator, "no previous case had involved a regulation that so substantially limited the use of property and had such substantial evidence that the zoning was intended to provide the public with a beach or to make acquisition of the property less expensive."[12] Nonetheless, the court found that the plaintiffs had failed to prove that there were no beneficial uses allowed by the ordinance. Indeed, the plaintiff's case was weak in this area, since they produced no evidence as to the effect of the ordinance on the value of the property, and had in fact previously requested a classification for commercial use. And the court disposed of the "bad faith" argument by finding that no evidence had been introduced to support such a contention, and that motives are not generally within the scope of judicial inquiry anyway. With regards the 'taking' question, there were essentially two classes of evidence available to justify the ordinance as a valid police power exercise. First, the planning consultants testified that the district was part of a comprehensive zoning scheme which sought balanced uses of properties in the city; that the beachfront property was eminently suited for recreation;

12. Hagman, Urban Planning and Land Development Control Law, at 215 (1971).

that the zoning classification was designed to take advantage of this unique natural resource; and that residential use would be unreasonable due to the high cost of construction and the depreciation of property values behind plaintiff's property. The second line of argument relied on more traditional grounds. There was evidence that the property was completely inundated during certain storms; that residences would have to be constructed on pilings; and that the safety of such construction was fairly debatable. In addition, the chief of police testified that illicit and immoral activities could take place under the pilings, causing a police problem. In its decision, the court relied on the latter of these classes of arguments and upheld the ordinance.

In sum, the rationale of the decision was a mixture of deference to legislative judgement on matters that are fairly debatable; strict enforcement of the rule that the burden of proof is on the landowner to establish a regulation as unreasonable; and reliance on convential police power objectives related to public health and safety. While it may be aruged that the case is an invaluable precedent in beach zoning cases where some beneficial use is possible, the court unfortunately did not deal directly with the propriety of an exclusive beach recreation zone. As one commentator has put it:

> ... consideration should not have been limited to the reasonableness of residential use of the property. In other words, the question of the case should have been: "May the city validly impose such a restriction?" rather than "May the city prohibit the building of residences on the land in question?" The court's failure to

> treat explicitly the former (broader)
> question leads to the underlying ambiguity
> of the holding. On the one hand, the
> court could be saying that so long as the
> owner is left with an assumed profitable
> use, the restriction to recreation use is
> valid. On the other hand, the court pro-
> bably is merely saying that under the cir-
> cumstances and for convential police power
> reasons, it was not improper to prohibit
> the building of residences on the beach
> property... It would be foolhardy to rely
> with assurance on the McCarthy case as in-
> dicating unequivocal judicial acceptance
> of recreation zoning wherever the owner
> can make a profit from the restricted use
> and the restriction is imposed as part of
> a comprehensive plan ....[13]

While these observations are well-taken, it does seem plausible that the three-fold rationale of McCarthy (defer-ence to legislative judgement; some reasonable use allowed; connection to public safety and welfare) could serve as a rational guideline for future judicial review of beach rec-reation districts or similar forms of exclusive use zoning for the protection of littoral open space. In the first place, it is useful to ask what distinguishes McCarthy from cases such as Vernon Park where exclusive use zones have been disallowed. The answer seems to lie in the courts willingness to maintain for the municipality a degree of flexibility in dealing with the complicated process of pro-tecting unique natural resources (as opposed to parking lots) and allocating them among competing public and private uses. If the McCarthy decision is read as it very well

---

13. Heyman, "Open Space and the Police Power", Open Space and the Law, Institute of Government Studies, Univ. of California (Berkeley), at 16 (Herring ed., 1965).

might be, to encourage limited judicial interference with government in its role of correcting for market imperfections where valuable environmental assets such as the shoreline are concerned, it is indeed an important precedent. Second, we should point out that the other rationales in McCarthy can be considerably strengthened when applied to different circumstances. In McCarthy, it turned out that the entire property of the plaintiffs came under the ordinance, whereas in other situations it might be possible to zone only that portion of the shorefront lot which lies below the vegetation line, such that the remaining land is still useful for residential and other private use. Furthermore, if ordinances can be related to traditional public safety factors (erosion, flooding, etc.) the rationale is strengthened even more.

Even in cases where the "unsafe use" rationale does not apply, it may be possible to substitute certain aesthetic considerations to restrict construction near the water's edge. Through the years courts have shown increased willingness to sanction aesthetic considerations, especially in scenic natural areas.[14] Consider the words of the Massachu-

---

14. See, e.g., Walker v. Board of County Commissioners, discussed supra, at p.174. A good example of undesirable beach construction from an aesthetic point of view is indiscriminate wharfing out in tidal areas. Albert Garreston, in a study of legal problems in the land-sea interface, found that a number of coastal communities are applying the special zoning district concept to their distinctive tidelands areas in order to regulate certain private activities within the context of a comprehensive overall plan. See Garreston, The Land Sea Interface of the Coastal Zone of the United States: Legal Problems Arising out of Multiple Use and Conflicts of Private and Public Interests, New York University, at 41 (1968).

setts Supreme Court:

> Grandeur and beauty of scenery contribute
> highly important factors to the public
> welfare of a state. To preserve such
> landscape from defacement promotes the
> public welfare and is a public purpose...
> It is, in our opinion, within the reason-
> able scope of the police power to pre-
> serve from destruction the scenic
> beauties bestowed upon the Commonwealth
> by nature....[15]

Coastline landscapes are among the most outstanding visual
resources in the nation. The very sharp edge of the
land-sea interface combined with immediately adjacent landforms and landscape units create visual panoramas that are
almost universally recognized as of high quality. Yet it is
along the coasts that are found the greatest number of landscape misfits--products of intensive and irresponsible development, in particular around major cities.

2.2   Flood Plain Zoning The primary purpose of establishing
a flood plain district is to protect the public health and
safety, and persons and property, against the hazards of
flood water inundation, as well as to protect the community
against the costs which may be incurred when unsuitable development occurs in swamplands, marshes, along watercourses,
and in other areas subject to floods.[16] Regulations which

---

15. General Outdoor Advertising Co. v. Dept. of Public
Works, 289 Mass. 149, 185-187, 193 N.E. 799, 815-816 (1935),
appeal dismissed, 297 U.S. 725.

16. See, e.g., Turnpike Realty v. Town of Dedham, 284 N.E.
2d 891, at 894 (Mass. 1972). For an extensive discussion of
flood plain zoning, see Dunham, "Flood Control via the Police Power", 107 U. Pa. L. Rev. 1098 (1959).

bar construction of most types of buildings in areas prone to flooding in effect reserve such areas exclusively for open space use, and this usually includes outdoor recreation. Permitted uses in flood plains often include parks, playgrounds, marinas or boat landings, and wildlife sanctuaries, and sometimes recreation and related open space uses are listed explicitly among the purposes of a flood plain ordinance.[17] Since many coastal areas are extremely susceptible to flooding hazards due to the action of waves and storm tides,[18] flood plain zoning is clearly an appropriate device for regulating shoreline developments, and has the attractive incidental benefit of maintaining certain areas in a condition supportive of future public recreational pursuits.

The decisions of the courts with respect to the constitutional validity of flood plain regulations are mixed, but seem to indicate that carefully drafted ordinances can generally withstand the test of judicial scrutiny. The prevention of public harm is by far the most compelling rationale

---

17. Purposes incidental to those related to the protection from the hazards of flooding include the conservation of natural conditions (e.g. ground water table), the protection of wildlife, and the maintenance of open spaces for agriculture, education, recreation, and general welfare of the public. See Turnpike Realty v. Town of Dedham, note 16 supra, at 894. In Turner v. County of Del Norte 24 Cal. App. 3d 311 (1972), the court held that an ordinance prohibiting residential or commercial structures on a flood plain, and limiting its use to parks, recreation, and agriculture, did not constitute an unlawful taking of property and was within the police powers of the local planning board.

18. For a case study of a coastal community ravaged by storm, see McHarg, Design with Nature, at 16-17 (1969).

for approval of such ordinances, especially in situations where floods have caused great property damage in the past. For example, in <u>Vartelas v. Water Resources Commission</u>[19], the Connecticut Supreme Court upheld a regulation establishing an encroachment line along a river because "the loss of human life and the destruction of property wrought by the floods in August, 1955, justified the legislature in conferring upon the Commission broad powers to adopt preventive measures against their repetition."[20] In this case, the regulation made all development impossible, but a later Connecticut ruling made it clear that such a severe denial of use would not be allowed without a clear and pressing flood hazard. In <u>Dooley v. Town Plan and Zone Commission of Town of Fairfield</u>[21], the Court invalidated a flood plain classification of plaintiffs land because much of the property was on high ground (untouched during a previous hurricane) and because the regulation resulted in a 75 percent depreciation in the value of the land. This the Court found unreasonable, in part because it all but restricted the potential buyers of the property to town or governmental agencies con-

---

19. 146 Conn. 650, 153 A. 2d 822 (1959).

20. Id. See also Turner v. County of Del Norte, 24 Cal. App. 3d 311 (1972), upholding an ordinance passed in connection with a regional flood control program initiated after a severe flood in 1964. Cases from other jurisdictions are cited in Bosselman et al., <u>The Taking Issue,</u> at 151, n. 33 (1973).

21. 151 Conn. 304, 197 A. 2d 770 (1964). See also Sturdy Homes Inc. v. Township of Redford, 30 Mich. App. 53, 186 N.W. 2d 43 (1971), where the court struck down a flood plain ordinance because the plaintiffs land had not been shown to be subject to flooding.

cerned with the provision of facilities for public use.
This points to another traditional concern of the courts,
i.e., that the police power may be improperly used to effectuate objectives usually associated with the exercise of
eminent domain. For example, in Baker v. Planning Board of
Framingham[22], the court reversed a planning board decision
to disapprove a subdivision plan so that the town could continue to use the owner's land as a water storage area to
avoid the extra cost of handling sewage and surface drainage
produced by the subdivision. And in Morris County Land Improvement Company v. Parsippany-Troy Hills Township[23], the
New Jersey Supreme Court invalidated an ordinance limiting a
portion of a swamp to agricultural, outdoor recreational,
and public utility uses on the grounds that the prime objective of the regulation was to retain the land substantially in its natural state for water retention and open
space preservation.[24]

All this emphasizes the importance of having a flood
plain ordinance fully supported by valid considerations of
public welfare, e.g. protection of individuals, land owners,
and the community from disasters, protection of prospective
buyers from unscrupulous real estate practices, etc. In
many cases, the desire to obviate potential hazards to the
public will outweigh the restriction of reasonable uses; and

---

22. 353 Mass. 141, 228 N.E. 2d 831 (1967).

23. 40 N.J. 539, 193 A. 2d 232 (1963).

24. "It is equally obvious from the proofs, and legally of
the highest significance, that the main purpose of enacting
regulations with the practical effect of retaining the mea-
dows in their natural state was for a public benefit." Id.,
at 240.

any additional purposes such as conserving natural conditions, wildlife, or recreational open spaces will not usually bring the regulatory measure into conflict with constitutionally protected private rights.[25]

3. Building Setbacks and Official Mapping

Since the real purpose of land-use controls in shoreline areas is to prevent construction which precludes future public use, it may not be necessary to designate recreation as an exclusive use. In the case of beaches and other relatively narrow coastal landforms, a simpler and less controversial approach which has the same ultimate effect would be to establish building setback lines, a land-use control established as a valid exercise of the police power in Gorieb v. Fox.[26] Here again, there is an advantage to regulating only a portion of the littoral property. As one commentator has noted:

> Building lines, encroachment lines, floodway limits, buffer zones, and other types of restrictions which severely restrict construction of structural uses on relatively narrow strips of land present less critical constitutional problems than similar regulations which restrict development in broader areas, since these generally affect only a portion of each lot and portions remain available for construction.[27]

---

25. See cases cited supra, note 17, at p. 172.

26. 274 U.S. 603 (1927).

27. Kusler, "Open Space Zoning: Valid Regulation or Invalid Taking," 57 Minn. L. Rev. 1, at 54 (1972).

Setback lines have been approved in furtherance of all the
traditional zoning objectives, including provision of light,
air, privacy, and yard space for lawns and trees; reduction
of fire hazards, safety hazards, and street congestion; maintenance of the general attractiveness of property and the
home environment.[28] In addition, aesthetic factors have been
explicitly recognized as important elements in the adoption
of setback requirements. In People v. Stover,[29] it was
stated that aesthetics may be an essential purpose in the establishment of setback lines. Thus, it seems that the application of building setback regulations to shoreline situations would be relatively straightforward. In Speigle v.
Beach Haven,[30] the New Jersey Supreme Court upheld an ordinance which prohibited construction and excavation between
the mean water line and a building line (with certain exceptions related to access and beach protection) in order to
protect beaches and dunes from erosion that would lead to
property damage from waves and storm tides. The court rejected the argument that the ordinance deprived the lands of
any beneficial use on the grounds that the plaintiffs did not
make a sufficient showing that they could make a safe and economic use of the land in question. Generally, the courts
seem to look at the entire property to determine if a reasonable use is possible; but in cases where setback lines leave

---

28. See cases cited in Note, "Zoning: Setback Line: A Reap-
praisal", 10 William and Mary L. Rev. 739, at 744 (1969).

29. 240 N.Y. 2d 734, 191 N.E. 2d 272 (1963).

30. 46 N.J. 479, 218 A. 2d 129 (1966); But see also King V.
Ocean Beach, 207 Misc. 100, 136 N.Y.S. 2d 690 (Sup. Ct.
1954), where a zoning ordinance which excluded all
construction from a buffer zone was invalidated.

no buildable space, the restriction will most likely be in-validated.[31]

Official maps are somewhat different from building lines in that they reflect a municipality's decision to locate streets, parks, and other facilities at places marked on the map. The maps are utilized to prevent construction which may add to future condemnation costs.[32] To avoid the criticism that such a regulation is unconstitutional on its face, a number of jurisdictions have added a "shock absorber" clause which allows a landowner to improve mapped areas if he can show that the property cannot yield a fair return under the mapped restrictions.[33] Conceivably, such an enactment could apply to shoreline areas that a governmental agency plans to acquire at some future date. However, the application of of-ficial mapping techniques to park and open space situations has been hampered by objections to the duration of restric-tions on development. In New Jersey, for example, mapping prohibitions for parks and playgrounds are limited to one year.[34] And in Miller v. City of Beaver Falls,[35] the Pennsylvania Supreme Court struck down a statute which pro-

31. See Kusler, op. cit. note 27 supra, at 56.

32. Official mapping appears to be the only device approved for this objective. See discussion and cases cited in Kus-ler, op. cit. note 27, supra, at 55.

33. See N.Y. Gen City Law, s. 35; Wisc. Stat. Ann. s. 62.23 (6) (1957).

34. See discussion in Krasnowiecki and Paul, "The Preserva-tion of Open Spaces in Metropolitan Areas", U. Penna. L. Rev. 179, at 186 (1961).

35. 368 Pa. 189, 82 A. 2d 34 (1951).

hibited for three years all incompatible development in areas
mapped for future parks. Nevertheless, a carefully designed
shore mapping ordinance could conceivably preserve coastal
open space areas for near-term acquisition for public recreation use.

4. Other Techniques

4.1 Subdivision Exaction
Under typical state enabling leg-
islation, a municipality may require that developers obtain
approval from a local planning board prior to subdivision of
property. Furthermore, the municipality is authorized to require as a condition of plat approval that the landowner provide or dedicate to public use such facilities as roads and
sewers,[36] or land for park or school purposes.[37] The general
rationale for such a requirement in the case of schools and
parks was put forth in Jordan v. Village of Menomonee Falls:

> The basis for upholding a compulsory land
> dedication requirement is this: the
> municipality by approval of a proposed
> subdivision plot enables the subdivider
> to profit financially by selling the sub-
> division lots as home building sites and
> thus realizing a greater price than could
> be obtained if he had sold his property
> as unplotted lands. In return for this
> benefit the municipality may require him
> to meet a demand to which the municipal-
> ity would not have been put but for the

36. See Ayres v. City Council, 34 Cal. 2d 31, 207 P. 2d 1
(1949); Newton v. American Sec. Co. 201 Ark. 943, 148 S.W.
2d 34 (1941).

37. See Zayas v. Planning Board, 69 P.R.R. 27 (1948); Bill-
ings, Properties, Inc. v. Yellowstone County, 144 Mont. 25,
394 P. 2d 182 (1964).

>influx of people into the community to
>occupy the subdivision lots.[38]

Thus local boards may force developers to bear part of the
cost of providing parks for outdoor recreation for new residents; but where the need for such services is a general one
not specifically attributable to the existence of the subdivision, the town usually must bear the cost. In the case of
exaction for street dedication, on the other hand, this distinction between the needs of subdivision residents and the
public at large may not be followed. In Ayres v. City Council, the court declared that "potential as well as present
population factors affecting the subdivision and the neigh-
borhood generally are appropriate for consideration"[39] by a
planning board in their projections of future traffic flow
over new streets.

In the case of subdivision in coastal areas, it has been
suggested that a requirement that developers dedicate public
easements for shore access where the subdivision would block
existing or potential access would fit within the existing
statutory framework.[40] The rationale is as follows:

>Requiring beach access is analogous to
>requiring streets of the width made ne-
>cessary by a city-wide traffic flow.

---

38. 28 Wis. 2d 608, 137 N.W. 2d 442 (1965), appeal dismissed
385 U.S. 4 (1966). See also Johnston, "Constitutionality of
Subdivision Control Exactions: The Quest for a Rationale",
52 Cornell L. R. 871, at 917 (1967); Pioneer Trust and
Savings Bank v. Village of Mount Prospect, 22 Ill. 2d 375,
176 N.E. 2d 799 (1961).

39. 34 Cal. 2d 31, at 41 (1949).

40. Note, "Public Access to Beaches," 22 Stanford L. Rev. 5,
at 568-569 (1970).

> While it is true that most of the demand
> for access comes from areas outside the
> subdivision, the existence of the subdi-
> vision aggravates the beach-access prob-
> lem. First, it may cut off exsiting ac-
> cess to beaches; second, even where no
> access preveiously existed, the new deve-
> lopment will raise land values and create
> a pattern of land use that will make it
> more difficult and expensive to purchase
> beach easements in the future.[41]

While this rationale seems plausible in situations where land
to be dedicated is to be used for access purposes, it seems
doubtful whether the argument can be extended to the use of
the shorefront itself, in which case it would be difficult to
establish the rational nexus between the exaction and the
public needs created by the subdivision development.

4.2 Compensable Regulations   An approach similar in effect to
the purchase of development rights in open space areas would
be to regulate and then make compensation available to certain landowners for losses suffered.[42] Under such a scheme,
the full market value of land prior to the imposition of regulations is guaranteed to the landowner if the regulation is
held to be invalid as a taking.[43] To the extent that the restrictions impair the value of the land for present uses,

---

41. Id., at 571.

42. See Krasnowiecki and Paul, "The Preservation of Open
Space in Metropolitan Areas", 110 U. Pa. L. Rev. 179 (1961).
See also Krasnowiecki and Strong, "Compensable Regulations
for Open Space", 24 J. of the Amer. Inst. of Planners, 87
(1963).

43. See, e.g., the scheme proposed in Tentative Draft #3,
American Law Institute Model Land Development Code, sec.
9-111 (3).

compensation is due immediately. To the extent that the potential development value of the property is reduced, the
owner is awarded damages at the time of sale equal to the
difference between the actual sale price and the original,
guaranteed value. Such a plan is thought to have a number of
advantages over acquisition of the fee simple or lesser interests in property such as easements. In the first place,
funds need not be expended unless and until a court finds
that the regulation would constitute a taking in the absence
of compensation.[44] And when expenditures are necessary, the
initial cost is relatively low since landowners do not recoup
lost development value until the property is actually sold;
and subsequent increases in the value of the land do not affect the ultimate cost to government, which is based on the
value prior to regulation.[45]

Compensable regulations have another attractive feature in
that they can enable a regulation enacted for a valid purpose
to remain effective:

> In substance, a system of compensable
> regulations is a means of validating land
> use regulations that are so restrictive
> that the courts would hold them to be a
> taking in the absence of compensation
> paid to the landowner. If enough compen-
> sation is paid to avoid the unconstitu-
> tionality then the regulation remains
> valid. In effect compensable regulations
> attempt to steer a middle course between
> regulation under the police power and

---

44. "Unlike programs of land acquisition which require large
quantities of front money, programs of compensable regulation postpone payment until after the need for payment has
been determined. And...the need may be decreasing." Bosselman, et al., op. cit. note 20 supra, at 305.

45. Krasnowiecki and Paul, op. cit. note 42 supra, at
199-202.

> taking under eminent domain.... (Whereas)
> traditional legal doctrines rarely allow
> the court to strike a middle ground by
> awarding the landowner such compensation
> as is necessary to prevent the regulation
> from being held unconstitutional.[46]

The compensable regulation approach seems well suited to the shoreline situation as an adjunct to other open space regulatory measures, since "provisions to compensate property owners can be of substantial benefit in assuring that achievement of a desirable end does not offend constitutional or other requirements of fairness."[47] However, the technique is virtually untested to date, and a number of disadvantages have been suggested. For example, some commentators feel that compensative schemes are subject to a greater range of administrative problems than are traditional acquisition programs.[48] Perhaps more significant, courts have tended to give considerable weight to speculative increases in land values when deliberating a 'taking' issue,[49] and compensable regulations might be challenged on the basis that they are

---

46. Bosselman, et al. op. cit. note 20 supra, at 302-303. See also Tentative Draft No. 5, American Law Institute Model Land Development Code, sec. 4-205 (1973), where the proposed code would authorize local governments to compensate wherever necessary to achieve the objectives of permissable regulation.

47. National Commission on Urban Problems, Building an American City, 251 (1968). The commission suggests that localities might well experiment with compensation regulation on a limites basis, e.g. by allowing it only for aesthetic and open space regulations.

48. See, e.g., Eveleth, "An Appraisal of Techniques to Preserve open Space," 9 Villanova L. Rev. 550, at 571 (1964).

49. See Kusler, op. cit. note 27 supra, at 79.

designed to depress land values to lower future condemnation
costs, a practice of which the courts are very wary.[50] Once
again, this emphasizes the importance of specifying valid
regulatory objectives (e.g. public safety, aesthetics, etc.)
when applying open space control techniques in coastal situations.

4.3 Tax Techniques   A number of commentators have suggested
that certain tax techniques be used in conjunction with land
use regulations and other schemes to preserve open spaces,
both as a means of compensation for reduced value and because
present taxation policies may tend to undercut otherwise
sound public policy measures. In the case of exclusive use
zoning and other potentially restrictive land-use controls,
tax adjustments which take into account the reduced development value of regulated lands could be used to ease the financial burden imposed on the landowner.[51]   Such a plan has
recently been proposed for the Lake Tahoe, Nevada area, where
the bi-state Regional Planning Agency has applied use restrictions to properties classified as 'general forest' and
'recreational.'   In response to pressures from landowners
whose property development potential was severely reduced, an
environmental tax credit has been devised which provides a 4
per cent annual tax credit on the federal income of affected

50. See Note, "Techniques for Preserving Open Spaces", 75
Harv. L. Rev. 1622, at 1640 (1962). See also the discussion
infra, at p.196.

51. See Kusler, op. cit. note 27 supra, at 73.   See also
Moore, "The Acquisition and Preservation of Open Lands", 23
Wash. & Lee L. Rev. 274, at 291 (1966).

individuals over a 25 year period. At the end of that time,
the land would be turned over to the federal government; thus
the plan is also seen as a relatively painless way for the
federal government to acquire public lands for future generations. Another suggested means for utilizing tax techniques
to complement other tools of public policy is to encourage
gifts of open space land through real estate tax conces-
sions.[52] Also, it has been suggested that permitting landowners to treat compensation received for development rights
as capital gains instead of ordinary income would encourage
the voluntary sale of easements to government.[53] All of
these schemes for preferential tax treatment would be applicable in coastal situations, and seem justifiable on the
grounds that they are designed to help attain public purposes
which are within the discretion of the legislature to promote
thorough use of the tax power.[54]   On the other hand, they
have been criticized on the grounds that the use of the tax
power as a tool of social policy detracts from its effectiveness as a generator of municipal revenues.[55] This creates a
number of political and administrative problems, a full ela-
boration of which is beyond the scope of this report.

---

52. Eveleth, op. cit. note 48, supra, at 574.

53. Delogu, "The Taxing Power as a Land Use Control Device",
45 Denver L. J. 279, at 285 (1968).

54. See Note, op. cit. note 50, supra, at 1641.

55. See Walker, "Loopholes in State and Local Taxes", 30
Tax Policy 4 (Feb. 1963).

5. Designing a Regulatory Strategy

It is evident from the foregoing discussion that a wide variety of regulatory techniques might be effectively applied to
the preservation of unique coastal areas as open spaces. The
purposes of such open-space regulations seem to fall within
the scope of the general welfare; and many courts have shown
substantial deference to legislative judgement together with
a willingness to strictly enforce the rule that the burden of
proof is on the landowner to demonstrate the unreasonableness
of regulatory measures. In addition, the particular nature
of the shoreline situation is such that non-compensable open
space regulations are likely to be validated on a number of
grounds. When the techniques for shoreline preservation such
as those outlined in this chapter are examined in relation to
the factors considered by the courts in determining whether
or not a 'taking' exists in particular open space cases, the
result seems favorable. With regards the prevention of public harm, regulations which prohibit construction below the
vegetation line are often supportable on grounds of public
safety, aesthetics, and ecological considerations. With regards the infringement on private property rights, non-compensable regulation may have less to commend it since the
natural characteristics of recreational shoreline may inherently limit its value to residential or some commercial uses,
thereby increasing the probability that the land will be
rendered valueless if frozen in its natural state.[56] However, we have noted that controls over the use of the water-

---

56. See Fonoroff, "Special Districts: A Departure from the
Concept of Uniform Controls", The New Zoning: Legal, Administrative, and Economic Concepts and Techniques, at 86 (Marcus & Groves ed. 1970).

front need not preclude relatively normal uses of upland
portions of littoral property. While there may be a substantial diminution of value as a result of such controls,
the courts often tend to give greater consideration to the
range of reasonable uses that are left unobstructed for the
property as a whole.[57] Moreover, even when severe use restrictions do threaten to invalidate a regulatory measure as
an unconstitutional taking, provisions for compensation may
serve as a convenient "safety valve" to preserve the integrity of the regulatory objectives sought.

The above observations indicate that open space ordinances regulating use of the seashore stand a good chance of
weathering constitutional storms with regards the issue of
taking without due process. Nevertheless, there are some
potential weaknesses in regulatory schemes that require
careful draftsmanship if they are to survive challenge in
court.[58] In particular, the courts are very sensitive to
situations where governments have traditionally paid to secure public use and then attempt in later instances to
achieve the same results through non-compensable regulation.
Another practice of which the courts are wary is the use of
regulatory controls designed to lower future condemnation or
purchase costs. Although not generally inclined to inquire
into motives, the courts will examine the circumstances surrounding a given regulation to see whether or not it was de-

---

57. This contention is supported by the conclusion of the
most recent study of the taking issue, where the popular
"myth" that land value cannot be severely reduced through
regulation was found to be unjustified by actual court decisions. See Bosselman, et al., op. cit. note 20 supra, at
328.

58. For an extensive discussion of the need for careful
draftsmanship, see Bosselman, Id., at 294 et seq.

signed to lower or preclude future costs rather than to serve some legitimate regulatory purpose.[59] As one commentator has noted:

> A regulation which restricts the use of private property solely to governmental functions, such as use for public schools, public parks, or public housing, as a prelude to later eminent domain proceedings, is uniformly regarded as an unconstitutional infringement of private property rights. Even in the absence of a limitation of public activities, highly restrictive use regulations imposed for the purpose of preventing private developments that would increase the cost of planned future acquisition of the subject property for governmental purposes, are equally invalid.[60]

All this suggests that a regulatory strategy for shoreline preservation should be carefully drawn with respect to both the purposes envisioned and the uses allowed. First, regulation of beaches and other shore recreation resources should be framed in terms of current and evolving police power objectives (safety, open spaces, etc.) without emphasizing the possibility of future acquisition for public use. Since the objectives of providing recreational opportunities and preventing resource despoilation or public harm are often compatible along the coastal strip, recreational

---

59. See Hagman, op. cit. note 12, supra, at 188; Grand Trunk W. Ry v. City of Detroit, 326 Mich. 387, 40 N.W. 2d. 195 (1949); 2700 Irving Park Bldg. Corp. v. City of Chicago, 395 Ill. 138, 69 N.E. 2d 827 (1946); Galt v. Cook County, 405 Ill. 396, 91 N.E. 2d. 395 (1950).

60. Van Alstyne, "Taking or Damaging by Police Power: The Search for Inverse Condemnation Criteria", 44 So. Cal. L. Rev. 1, at 23 (1971).

purposes can be served without being made explicit, or at least without being held up as the primary concern. Second, permitted uses should be as varied as possible, for "the more that a landowner is allowed to make use of his property, the less he is likely to raise a taking issue."[61] Furthermore, the allowed development should be as private as possible in the sense that it allows the owner some chance of a reasonable economic use.[62] In one sense, the more attractive a coastal location is for public recreational use, the higher is the potential return to the owner if he collects user fees or other service charges. In the McCarthy[63] case discussed previously, where a town's classification of plaintiff's property as a beach recreation district was obviously designed to maintain public use of the beach, the court noted that the regulation did not prevent the owner from fencing off the area and charging an entrance fee, and this factor helped persuade the court to uphold the ordinance.

A final consideration that is important to the success of any shoreline regulation strategy with regards the taking

---

61. "If strict performance standards are applied to the use of the land the careful draftsman often finds that many more types of development could be permitted than an initial reaction might have suggested." Bosselman, op. cit. note 20 supra, at 294.

62. A good illustration of activities that might be offered to establish the economic "rent" value of a salt marsh or of a restricted coastal area of scenic beauty can be found in Wilkes, "Constitutional Dilemmas Posed by State Policies Against Marine Pollution--The Maine Example", 23 Maine L. Rev. 143, at 152 (1971).

63. McCarthy v. City of Manhattan Beach, 41 Cal. 2d 879, 264 P. 2d 932 (1953).

issue is the persuasiveness of technical evidence presented
to the courts.[64] Careful factual preparation is often the
deciding variable in the intangible balancing process. In
Speigle v. Borough of Beach Haven[65], for example, the New
Jersey Supreme Court upheld a setback line for dune protection because the borough produced "unrebutted proof that it
would be unsafe to construct houses oceanward of the building line...because of the possibility that they would be destroyed during a severe storm--a result which occurred
during the storm of March, 1962."[66]

6. Concluding Remarks

It seems incontrovertible at this point that a variety of
regulatory techniques can play a vital role in preserving
(and to some extent providing) open space opportunities for
public recreation along the coastal shoreline of the United
States. That they have not done so in the past is attributable in part to the fact that open space and related objectives haven't been universally accepted, or at least the opposition has been an extremely vocal and influential minority
that makes good use of the "myth" that all regulation which
restricts the use of property is an unconstitutional taking
without compensation. In any event, when passing on controversial open space regulations, the courts hesitate to substitute their judgement for that of the state legislatures
as to what are reasonable means to worthy ends, and they
often look for strong enabling legislation to legitimize

---

64. For an extensive discussion, see Bosselman, op. cit.
note 20 supra, at 284 et seq.

65. 46 N.J. 479, 218 A. 2d 129 (1966).

66. Id., 218 A. 2d, at 137 (1966).

emerging objectives. Such legislation has not been generally available with regards shoreline recreational use;
aside from the Texas and Oregon statutes discussed in
Chapter 7, state legislation to protect public rights in the
uplands portion of the coastal shorelines has been enacted
in only a few states. In Washington, a 1901 statute declared that the state's foreshore was a public highway,[67]
and in 1963 this highway was extended to the vegetation line
and declared to be a public recreation area.[68] In Hawaii, a
1970 statute mandated the Land Use Commission to establish
setback areas of between 20 and 40 feet from the edge of vegetation growth. Also, counties are authorized to extend the
setback areas further inland if appropriate,[69] and much of
the land seaward of the vegetation line has been placed in
Conservation Districts.[70] Finally, both Wisconsin and California[71] have enacted subdivision regulations governing
shorefront developments which require the provision of access for the use of tidelands or the water. Apart from
these statutes, in the past the courts have had to rely on

---

67. R.C.W.A. 79 16.170-171.

68. Wash. Laws, 1963, ch. 212.

69. Act 136 - 1971. Hawaii also has a special statute which
prohibits the construction of a beach at Waikiki unless legal
arrangements are made to guarantee public use of any such
beach within 75 feet shoreward of the mean high water mark.
See Hawaii v. Willburn, 49 Hawaii 651, 426 P. 2d 626, at 628
(1967).

70. See Matter of the Application of Ashford, 76 P. 2d 440
(1968).

71. Cal. Bus. & Prof. Code, secs. 11610.5(a), 7 (a) (West
Supp. 1971).

very vague guidelines set forth in often outdated standard
zoning and planning enabling acts, and this has increased
the likelihood that land-use controls for seashore preservation would fail the judicial test of reasonableness.

There is evidence, however, that this situation is changing rapidly. Recent years have witnessed a flood of coastal
resource management activity at the state level, as programs
have been developed in the areas of wetlands preservation,
beach access, flood plain controls, shorelands zoning, site
location and regulation, comprehensive planning, and comprehensive management.[72] Some states have acted with a sense
of urgency to check the trends in coastal development while
state policy is formulated and debated in the legislature
and among the citizenry. For example, California voters
approved by referendum the now-famous "Proposition 20",
which prohibits any development in the area between the seaward limits of state jurisdiction and 1000 yards landward
from the mean high tide line, unless a permit has been ob-
tained from the newly-created state or regional coastal

---

72. See generally, Armstrong & Bradley, Description and
Analysis of Coastal Zone and Shoreland Management Programs in
the United States, U. of Michigan Sea Grant Program, Technical Report No. 20, (March 1972). Some examples of coastal
states which have enacted resource management laws are as
follows: California (San Francisco Bay Conservation and
Development Commission, coastal zone act); Delaware (coastal
zone act); Georgia (coastal marshlands); Maine (shoreland
zoning); Michigan (Great Lakes and flood plain protection);
Minnesota (shoreland development and flood plain controls);
New Jersey (wetlands, coastal zone); North Carolina (beach
erosion and coastal wetlands); Oregon (coastal zone); Rhode
Island (coastal resources management, intertidal salt marsh
and coastal wetlands protection); Virginia (wetlands);
Washington (coastline protection); Wisconsin (shoreland
zoning and flood plains).

conservation commission.[73]   In   other   states, land-use controls   such   as   the ones examined in this chapter are being
encouraged as the most   effective means to preserve and protect valuable coastal areas.   For example, Maine has enacted
a mandatory shoreland zoning law[74] which requires all municipalities to adopt   shoreland   zoning and subdivision ordinances.   The law further authorizes   state   review   of local
ordinances for consistency with comprehensive standards, one
of which calls for a building setback of 75   feet   from   the
water's edge.[75]

All this is part of a broader trend   that has been termed
a "quiet resolution in land   use   control",[76] which   is evidenced   by   numerous land use laws and legislative proposals
at both the state and federal levels.[77]   The thrust of these
efforts is toward establishing a   new   concept   which   holds
that land should be considered as a   resource and not merely

73. Proposition   No. 20, "Coastal Zone   Conservation Act",
Propositions and   Proposed Laws, General Election, Tuesday,
November 7, 1972, California.

74. 12 M.R.S.A. 4811-4814; See also 30 M.R.S.A. 4961-4962.

75. See University of Maine, Shoreland Zoning Project, "A
Summary of Interim Guidelines for Shoreline Zoning and Sub-
division", Environmental Studies Center, Univ. of Maine at
Orono (Oct. 1972).

76. See generally, Bosselman and Collies, The Quiet Revolution in Land-Use Control, US Council on Environmental Quality, Washington, D.C. (1971).

77. See generally, National Land Use Policy Legislation--
93rd Congress: An Analysis of Legislative Proposals and
State Laws, Committee on Interior and Insular Affairs,
United States Senate (April, 1973). See also "Land Use Policy and Planning Assistance Act," Report No. 93-197 of the
Committee on Interior and Insular Affairs, U.S. Senate, at
80-83 (1973).

a commodity; and that important social and environmental goals require more specific controls on the uses that may be made of scarce land resources. This dual concept of resource accountability and protection of "amenity" values is strongly reflected in the Coastal Zone Management Act of 1972, which calls for the "wise use of the land and water resources of the coastal zone, giving full consideration to ecological, cultural, historic, and aesthetic values as well as to needs for economic development."[78] Within the context of this new mood of environmental awareness, judicial attitudes toward what is a reasonable use of the police power to effectuate desired social ends seem to be undergoing a quiet revolution of their own;[79] and this bodes well for the use of regulatory measures to achieve open-space objectives in coastal areas.

---

78. P.L. 92-583, 86 Stat. 1280, sec. 303 (b). Another example of federal concern for the uniqueness of the coastal environment is the Nantucket Sound Islands Bills, introduced by Senator Kennedy and presently under consideration by the Congress (S. 1929, 93rd Congress, 2nd Sess., 1974).

79. See Candlestick Properties, Inc. v. San Francisco Bay Conservation and Development Commission, 89 Cal. Rptr. 897 (1970); Just v. Marinette County, 56 Wis. 2d 7, 201 N.W. 2d 761 (1972). For a discussion of this quiet judical revolution, see Bosselman, op. cit. note 20 supra, at 212 et seq.

Part III

CONCLUDING REMARKS AND APPENDICES

Chapter 11

THREE BASIC ISSUES IN COASTAL RESOURCE MANAGEMENT

1. Introduction

As indicated in the beginning of this report, the purpose has not been to arrive at a set of policies which might "solve" the shoreline recreation problem, but to set forth the means by which state government and/or their political subdivisions can effectuate appropriate management plans. Nor has there been any suggestion as to the most desirable mix of remedial techniques, because this will depend on the legal and political and practical circumstances surrounding any given resource base. There is, on the other hand, a deep-seated conviction embodied herein that coastal open spaces for public recreational use have been grossly and unjustifiably undervalued by the processes we have historically relied upon to allocate the shoreline among competing uses. This conviction is but a part of the larger concept that has emerged in recent years, that land and air and water should be viewed as resources rather than simply as commodities, and that governments at all levels are charged with a "trusteeship" to ensure their wise and beneficial use. Since these resources --especially land--are key threads in the fabric of economic and social activity, the proper exercise of this trust on the part of the public sector is clearly of enormous consequence. In the case of coastal resource management in general, and shoreline recreation in particular, there are some very important issues regarding the future role of collective (governmental) action with respect to resource allocation and protection, and this report cannot conclude without some general observations on each of these matters.

2. The Rationale for a New Mode of Collective Action

Decreasing open space for public recreational use is a proto-
typical coastal resource management problem because it calls
for new modes of collective action, in three respects.
First, in Chapter 4 it was seen that the organization of economic activity militates against the incorporation of amenity
values (such as those related to ecology, public recreation,
aesthetics, etc) into decision processes surrounding the allocation of coastal resources. Second, in Chapter 5 it was
asserted that the organization of political activity which
has traditionally been relied on to compensate for market deficiencies can also contribute to the misallocation of such
resources, particularly when decisions of more than local
significance are made solely on the basis of local needs and
values. Finally, the analysis in Chapter 9 suggested that
the organization of legal activity (i.e. current use of the
'taking' clause as the primary mechanism to resolve conflicts
between diffuse public interests and individual rights) posed
a number of constitutional difficulties for regulatory approaches designed to remedy the misallocation of open space
for public use in the coastal zone. These observations all
point to a need for government to begin to function in new
ways and at a higher level of consciousness in developing
coastal resource use policies whose sophistication matches
the complexity of the problems at hand.

Traditionally, collective action has functioned in a rather peripheral way with respect to market allocation of
coastal resources, as the historical division of resource
control responsibilities among levels of government has been
founded on concerns about the undue centralization of politi-

cal power rather than on considerations of efficiency in allocative decision processes. As long as there was plenty of
shoreline available to satisfy all the demands from competing
private uses while leaving adequate opportunities for public
activities, there was no perceived need to reassess the distribution of functions among the public and private sectors.
The public sector was content with acquiring and managing
public lands and otherwise adopting a laissez-faire posture
in setting the boundary constraints for private sector decisions.

But today, with the increasing concentrations of population and development in the coastal zone and the rapidly
diminishing supply of resources to accommodate the needs
attendant to this growth, deficiencies in this allocative
system have become more pronounced, especially in relation to
ecological and amenity uses (such as recreation, aesthetics,
historical and cultural preservation, etc.) As multiple
'spillover' effects have begun to emerge in these contexts,
we have become more cognizant of the interrelatedness of re-
source-use decisions and of the failure of existing institutional arrangements to deal with them properly. As a result,
governments in general are increasingly being called upon to
take a more direct role in providing for and protecting
qualitative, intangible coastal values left unattended by the
market; and the various levels of government are being called
upon to cooperate and coordinate their efforts in hopes of
fostering a broader perspective when dealing with resource
allocation problems cutting across legally-established jurisdictional lines. These changing roles for government in the
process of allocating scarce coastal resources are strongly
reflected in the Congressional findings in the Coastal Zone

Management Act of 1972:

> In light of the competing demands and the
> urgent need to protect and give high
> priority to natural systems in the coas-
> tal zone, present state and local insti-
> tutional arrangements for planning and
> regulating land and water uses in such
> areas are inadequate; and
>
> The key to more effective protection and
> use of the land and water resources of
> the coastal zone is to encourage the
> states to exercise their full authority
> over the lands and waters in the coastal
> zone by assisting the states, in cooper-
> ation with Federal and local governments
> and other vitally affected interests, in
> developing land and water use programs
> for the coastal zone, including unified
> policies, criteria, standards, methods,
> and processes for dealing with land and
> water use decisions of more than local
> significance.[1]

To this point, the discussion has focused on the economic
and political aspects of the new mode of governmental action, but the legal dimension is equally important. In the
past, the courts have subjected governmental regulations of
the use of land resources to more stringent tests than they
have to other forms of governmental regulation.[2] Histor-

---

1. Public Law 92-583, 86 Stat. 1280, secs. 302 (g), (h).
Enacted by the 92nd Congress, October 27, 1972. See Appendix A, infra, for full text of the Act.

2.   "While other regulations are only tested to determine
whether they bear a reasonable relationship to a valid public purpose, land use regulations must be tested by balancing the value of the regulation against the loss in value
to each affected property owner." Bosselman, Callies, and
Banta, The Taking Issue, at 238 (1973).

ically, these judicial criteria with respect to the exercise
of regulatory powers over land were intended primarily to
safeguard the rights of property owners against arbitrary
and unfair governmental action. But now it has become clear
that individual actions, taken together, may adversely affect diffusely-held public interests, and the courts are
being called upon to create a legal climate conducive to the
effective exercise of new governmental responsibilities to
protect these interests.

In sum, the development of effective coastal resource
management programs will involve three elements with respect
to the proper mode of government action. First, we must begin to reevaluate the interface between government and social values, because ecological and amenity objectives must
now be articulated and weighed in the absence of a
property-functioning market. Secondly, we must begin to reevaluate the interface between state and local governments,
because parochial decision-making by itself cannot achieve a
balanced use of the resource base that reflects regional
needs and concerns. And third, we must begin to reevaluate
the interface between the law and regulation by government,
because the nature of the public interest requires the evolution of more appropriate legal doctrines. The remainder
of this chapter will be devoted to a discussion of these
considerations insofar as they relate to the shoreline recreation situation.

3. State vs. Local Control

The first issue to be dealt with relative to open space and
recreational elements of coastal resource management pro-

grams is: How can a broader range of policy considerations be incorporated into decision processes at the local level, when the impacts of the decisions transcend jurisdictional lines? As we have seen, there has been a conspicuous absence of any regional perspective as to the value of open spaces for public recreational use in the coastal zone, as local political subdivisions have generally responded only to local concerns regarding maintenance of the property tax base, reservation of facilities for exclusive municipal use, etc. Futhermore, regulatory approaches to shoreline preservation have historically been least effective at the local level when political pressure for development is high, as is usually the case along the coastline. However, to put this in proper perspective, we should point out that a recent American Law Institute report has indicated that 90 per cent of the land-use decisions currently being made by local governments have little or no significant impact on state or national interests.[3] While this percentage is undoubtedly much higher in coastal areas where a greater portion of the resourses are of more than local value, there is no conclusive evidence to suggest that management by state fiat is required as a matter of a broad policy. Even though it is clear that many existing decision processes at sub-state levels are inadequate insofar as coastal resources are concerned, it does not follow that wholesale rejection of these processes is necessary. Although ultimate decision-making at the state level is desirable in some cases, the general rule should be that co-operation in good faith should come before pre-emption, i.e. the carrot before the stick.

---

3. American Law Institute, Model Land Development Code (Tent. Draft No. 3, 1971).

We should also note that, while local governments may tend
to allocate resources of regional significance solely on the
basis of local needs and values, this does not imply irrational behavior on their part, since a town government is
charged with protecting the interests of the town residents,
not the public at large. Even though their actions may be
inefficient and inequitable from the regional standpoint, we
must be cognizant of the undue burdens that might be placed
on both the resource base and on the coastal towns under alternative arrangements.   Clearly there is a need for a
broader perspective, but this perspective should not be allowed to arbitrarily preempt the legitimate concerns of the
coastal municipalities.

The federal coastal zone management law has suggested a
new framework of decision-making wherein the states are urged
to assume a more integral role vis-a-vis sub-state entities.[4]
Prior to granting approval of funding for state programs
under section 306 of the Coastal Zone Management Act of 1972,
the Secretary of Commerce must find that the program provides
for one or a combination of three control techniques, as
follows: (1) State establishment of criteria and standards
for local implementation, subject to administrative review
and enforcement of compliance; (2) Direct state land and
water use planning and regulation; or (3) State administrative review for consistency with the management program of
all development plans, projects, or land and water use regulations proposed by any state or local authority or private
developer, with power to approve or disapprove after public

---

4. For a general discussion of the emerging role of the
states in land-use decision processes, see Land Use   Policy
and Planning Assistance Act, Report No. 93-197 of the Committee on Interior Affairs, U.S. Senate (S.268--1973).

notice and an opportunity for public hearings.[5] An innovative precedent that seems to fall within this framework in
the case of shoreline recreation resources can be found in
the federal legislation establishing the Cape Cod National
Seashore in Massachusetts.   Instead of attempting to acquire
all the shorefront envisioned for the park, the Congress authorized the establishment of criteria to be followed by local towns within the proposed seashore area in the drafting
of land-use control ordinances.[6]   Not only did this obviate
the need for considerable expenditures by the federal government, it also enabled littoral properties to remain on the
local tax rolls.   In the event that compliance with the federal criteria was not forthcoming from a given town, the
Secretary of the Interior was authorized to acquire the
needed lands.   This formula seems to provide one means for
striking a workable balance between cooperation and coercion
as between the different levels of government involved.

4. Legal Constraints vs. Administrative Flexibility

The second issue of great importance to the effectiveness of
open space and recreational aspects of coastal resource management programs is the attitude taken by the courts in applying legal constraints to administrative action.   This has

---

5. P.L. 92-583, 86 Stat. 1280, sec. 306 (e), (1).

6. See generally, 16 U.S.C., s. 459b et seq. The towns of
Chatham, Provincetown, Truro, Wellfleet, Eastham, and Orleans
all have adopted the required land-use regulations. See e.g.,
Town of Chatham, Mass., Protective By-Laws, sec. 3.5 (Resi-
dence-Seashore Conservancy District 10 - 1969).

special significance in the case of regulatory approaches to
the preservation of unique shoreline recreation resources,
where the issue of taking without compensation may pose considerable difficulty. Historically, the criteria developed
by the courts in this regard were intended to safeguard the
rights of individual property owners against arbitrary, unfair, and tyrannical government action. Prof. Sax, in his
early article on the taking question,[7] argued that re-
source-acquisition through regulation by government presents
a three-fold source of danger: (1) the risk of discrimination ("the official procurement process provides a particularly apt opportunity for rewarding the faithful or pun-
ishing the opposition"); (2) the risk of excessive zeal
("government involved in pursuing an important national goal
... may be prone to display a questionable zeal in acquiring
the tools needed to get on with the job"); and (3) the risk
of excessive exposure to losses ("a good argument can be
made that the proper way to draw the line limiting exposure
to losses is with the distinction between the demands of
private competition and those of resource-seeking government
enterprises.").

While the above dangers will always exist, it has become
clear with the advent of the environmental movement that
more diffuse rights on the part of the general public require protection similar to that traditionally accorded to
private interests. Conventional notions of land-use spillovers affecting adjacent properties or an identifiable seg-
ment of the public at large have given way to a more sophis-

---

7. Sax, "Taking and the Police Power," 74 Yale L. J. 36, at
64-65 (1964).

icated understanding of the inter-connectedness of seemingly discrete resource uses. This has posed renewed difficulty for the courts, since the concept of "external harm" now clearly encompasses a broad range of public interests that are not always readily identifiable or quantifiable.

Faced with dilemmas of this sort, it becomes necessary to reconsider the notion of property rights as the central element in the regulation/taking issue. Such a reconsideration has, in fact, led Sax to a reformulation of his original theory:

> The abandon with which private resource users have been permitted to degrade our natural resources may be attributable in large measure to our limited conception of property rights. Not surprisingly, an amended notion of property rights suggests a reformulation of the law of takings. Perhaps more importantly, a new view of property rights suggests that current takings law stands as an obstacle to rational resource allocation.[8]

In disowning his original view that whenever government can be said to acquire resources on its own account, compensation must be paid, Sax asserts that much of what was formerly deemed a taking is better seen as an exercise of the police power in vindication of diffusely-held claims ("public rights") to a common resource base. These rights are in jeopardy when the use of property has spillover effects on

---

8. Sax, "Taking, Private Property, and Public Rights", 81 Yale L. J. 149, at 150 (1971).

other property interests,[9] and should be entitled to equal consideration in legislative or judicial resolution of conflicts that arise as a result of these spillovers. The purpose of public sector activity, then, "is to put competing resource-users in a position of equality when each of them seeks to make a use that involves some imposition (spill-over) on his neighbors ..."[10] Essentially, this recognizes that the roles of government as mediator and as participant in the economic system often overlap when conflicts arise between private interests and public rights. Government must seek to mediate these conflicts, but in doing so it must also represent those diffuse public interests which would otherwise be left ignored.[11] If the courts are to avoid disrupting the effectiveness of these processes, Sax feels they should confine their questions in determining whether or not compensation is due to: (1) whether or not an owner is being prohibited from making a use of his land that has no conflict-creating spillover effect; and (2) whether or not government is guilty of discriminatory action.[12] The great advantage of this approach is that it

---

9. Conflict-creating spillover effects are categorized as: 1) uses of property resulting in direct encumbrance on the uses of other property; 2) uses of a common to which others have an equal right; or 3) the use of property that affects the health or well-being of others. Id., at 162.

10. Id., at 161.

11. "The essence of a public rights . . . . approach to the question of takings should make clear that the government should vindicate the rights of taxpayers as a group as well as the rights of individual property owners." Id., at 171.

12. Id., at 176.

decouples the taking issue from any artificial categorization
of the modes of government activity (i.e. harm-preventing vs.
benefit-compelling). This allows government a greater flexibility in balancing diffusely-held claims vs. traditional
property interests, a complex task that the courts are probably ill-equipped to assume[13] and reluctant to engage in. At
the same time, courts can focus more explicitly on developing
rules to protect against governmental abuse of discretion.[14]
While Sax acknowledges that legislative decision-processes
are not always rational, he points out that the relevant
issue is whether conventional rules will make the process
more rational. But clearly they do not:

> ... the current takings scheme introduces
> an irrationality by requiring compen-
> sation when the conflict resolution sys-
> tem imposes extreme economic harm on dis-
> crete users but not when analoguous harm
> is placed on diffuse users. The proposed
> scheme has the advantage of making com-
> peting uses doctrinally equal, leaving
> their accommodation to be decided as a
> matter of public policy rather than of

---

13. At least one other commentator is convinced that balancing tests are too difficult for the courts to apply. See
Michelman, "Property, Utility, and Fairness: Comments on the
Ethical Foundations of Just Compensation", 80 Harv. L. Rev.
1165 (1967).

14. On the question of arbitrary and discriminatory government regulation, Sax analogizes to the judicial rules developed to prevent spot zoning. On the question of excessive
zeal in seeking broad social objectives, he points out that
the courts are greatly aided by political checks on decision-making processes which would not allow the "public interest" to routinely prevail over traditional private rights.
Sax, op. cit., note 8 supra at 170-171.

inflexible legal rules.[15]

These observations have important implications for the shoreline recreationa¹ situation. While the courts have substituted a balancing test for the traditional bene- fit-compelling vs. harm-preventing criteria in open space litigation, inevitably this balancing test will become too complex for the courts to deal with. How can the diminution in value of a regulated littoral property be compared within a legal context to the aestheic or recreational value gained for the public at large? Such trade-offs are meant for pol- itical and administrative processes, and the courts must de- velop a more sophisticated approach that can both maintain administrative flexibility while guarding against potential abuses of discretion. At the same time, governmental agen- cies faced with the possibility of litigation challenging the constitutionality of shoreline controls should adopt a strategy for approaching the taking issue which emphasizes careful draftsmanship, sound technical evidence, and which takes advantage of the trend toward increasing judicial ac- ceptance of open space and related environmental objec- tives.[16]

---

15. Id., at 172.

16. For an extensive discussion of these strategies see Bosselman, et. al., op. cit., note 2 supra, at 236 et seq. Alternative strategies also suggested therein include (1) a return to strict construction of the taking clause which limits the concept to an actual physical invasion by govern- ment; (2) adoption of legislative standards to codify more precisely the line between regulation and taking; and (3), avoiding the issue altogether by relying on acquisition and/or compensation programs such as those discussed earlier in this report.

5. Determining Priorities Among Uses

Having considered issues of organizational structure and relationships between different levels and branches of government, there remains a third and perhaps most fundamental
question with regards the management of coastal resources:
How should government go about reaching allocative decisions
involving social and economic impacts, when some groups gain
and other lose as a consequence of the choices made, and
when the values of different groups are in conflict? Among
the requirements of the federal Coastal Zone Management Act
are the provisions that federally-funded state management
programs must include "a definition of what shall constitute
permissable land and water uses within the coastal
zone"[17] and "broad guidelines on priority of uses in particular areas."[18] In other situations, the market system is
relied on to serve these functions because it provides a
simple, sure, and self-correcting process which will reflect
changes in social desires. But in the case of shoreline resources, the market has clear allocative imperfections, thus
providing a rationale for collective intervention. This reflects the expectation that governmental activity can, in
effect, take up where the market leaves off, bringing about
a distribution of coastal resources among competing uses
that is more representative of social values and more re-
sponsive to public needs.   The fulfillment of this expectation is the greatest challenge facing the states in the
development of coastal zone management programs.

---

17. P.L. 92-583, sec. 305 (b)(2).

18. P.L. 92-583, sec. 305 (b)(5).

To illustrate the nature of this task, consider the host
of practical issues raised by the suggestion that public recreational opportunities in the coastal zone be expanded.
This report has focused on the relatively narrow strip
centered about the land-sea interface, i.e. the recreational resource itself. The prospect of widespread public
use of any given resource, however, must be considered
within a much broader geographical and social context.[19] In
addition to a possible diminution in private enjoyment, more
public use could mean that more parking lots, transportation facilities, hotel and motel accommodations, and many
other recreation-related developments will be required in
the zones immediately adjacent to seashore areas. The effects of such development could reverberate throughout the
surrounding regions, bringing increased congestion and
greater police problems in areas already overburdened with
seasonal demands for municipal services. This raises questions concerning the equitable distribution of benefits and
costs, and what is the socially-optimal allocation of the
resource base. How much can the supply be increased before
significant disruptions in existing patterns of activity are
felt? This will depend to some extent on the availability
of new areas suitable for public use (e.g. abandoned mili-

19. For a discussion of factors in regional planning for
tourism, see Ketchum, ed., The Water's Edge, at 93 et seq.
(1973).

tary facilities[20] or artificial islands[21]); and on the crea-
tive application of flexible planning methods and advanced
management techniques to achieve compatible diversity of
uses. Beyond this, how are trade-offs to be identified and
evaluated, and at what point would further expansion of public opportunities be undesirable? In the first instance,
this will depend on the ecological capability of the resource to support development and/or use.[22] It will also
depend on a reliable evaluation of the opportunities lost
and the benefits gained by devoting additional resources to
public rather than private use. Finally, it will depend
somewhat on the range of recreational alternatives available
at inland facilities, and on the willingness of the public
to substitute other forms of recreation (e.g. backyard

20. A number of military-owned coastal locations have been
released for non-defense purposes in recent years, including
Governors Island in New York Harbor and Fort Totten on Long
Island Sound. Furthermore, the Defense Department has
announced the closing of many naval bases around the
country, and this is expected to open up significant new
opportunities for public recreation, mostly in urban
settings where the need is greatest.

21. For a discussion of techniques for shoreline development
and modification for optimal use, See Spangler, New Technology and Marine Resources Development, at 469-476 (1970).

22. See Schoenbaum, "Public Rights and Coastal Zone Management", 51 N. Car. L. Rev. 1, at 26-27 (1972). With regards
the ecological effects of recreational use, it has been suggested that leisure-home subdivision and similar high density private development can maximize use more efficiently
than public development. See Teclaff and Teclaff, "Saving
the Land-Water Edge From Recreation, For Recreation," 14
Arizona L. Rev. 39, at 60 (1972). See also Kusler,
"Artificial Lakes and Land Subdivisions," 1971 Wis. L. Rev.
369, at 370-373.

pools, etc.), or to travel greater distances to reach other coastal facilities.

The foregoing observations are not by any means intended to diminish the conviction that public recreational opportunities in the coastal shorelines are underproduced. The purpose is to indicate the complexity of adjusting the allocative system to correct such a situation without introducing additional disruptions that could counterbalance any benefits achieved. Therefore, if rational shoreline use policies are to be accomplished, the application of regulatory measures must be preceded by intelligible planning and must be related to a coherent framework for decision-making. These concepts are cornerstones of the federal Coastal Zone Management Act, which calls for a comprehensive approach to coastal allocation through the development of unified policies, criteria, standards, methods, and processes for dealing with land and water use decisions. This approach is reflected in the Act's definition of a management program:

> "Management program" includes, but is not limited to, a comprehensive statement in words, maps, illustrations, or other media of communication, prepared and adopted by the state in accordance with this title, setting forth objectives, policies, and standards to guide public and private uses of lands and waters in the coastal zone.[23] (Emphasis added)

With these words, the Congress has indicated that a more centralized process of land-use planning and control must be relied upon to establish priorities and effectuate ob-

---

23. P.L. 92-583, sec. 304(g).

jectives that the decentralized market could not. However,
we must recognize that the planning process is itself im-
perfect, and an appreciation for some of the potential difficulties of this approach is a prerequisite to the design
of coastal management programs.

The concept of planning assumes that an efficient allocation of resources based on social values can be achieved
if we employ the combined insights and learning of the
economist, the environmental designer, the sociologist, the
public health expert, the philosopher, and all other
professionals concerned with social problems. The planning
process is thought to be "a constantly evolving and continuously changing phenomenon--an evolutionary scheme which
through the medium of development policies is progressively
adjusted in the flow of time to take account of unpre-
dictable elements of technological and social
change."[24] During the late 1920's, the concept of planning
was first introduced on a national scale in The Standard
Planning Enabling Act[25] and the Standard Zoning Enabling
Act[26], prepared by the Department of Commerce and subsequently adopted by most states.   In their original form,
these Acts vested in city or regional planning commissions
the power to develop a 'master plan' with recommendations

24. Freilich, "Interim Development Controls: Essential
Tools for Implementing Flexible Planning and Zoning", J.
of Urban Law 65 (1971). See also Chapin, Urban Land Use
Planning, at 98 (2d ed. 1965).

25. U.S. Dept. of Commerce, Advisory Commission on City
Planning and Zoning, A Standard Planning Enabling Act
(1928).

26. U.S. Dept. of Commerce, Advisory Committee on City
Planning and Zoning, A Standard Zoning Enabling Act (1926).

as to the general location of public and private activities. The primary purposes in view were to protect the
health, safety, morals, and general welfare of society by
ensuring the orderly development of the community resource
base.   Towards these ends, local zoning boards have been
empowered to regulate and restrict the height and size of
buidings, the size of yards and other open spaces, the density of population, and the location and use of buildings,
structures and land for trade, industry, residence or other
purposes.   Originally, it was envisioned that zoning and
other land-use controls were merely tools by which the master plan could be implemented. However, for a variety of
reasons, the two concepts became separated, with zoning becoming widely accepted and with master planning--espe-
cially on a regional basis--never exerting important in-
fluences on urban or regional development on a broad
scale.[27] As one commentator has noted:

> ...we have been totally remiss in fail-
> ing to provide legal mechanisms to pro-
> tect and nourish the planning process
> and as a result we have almost totally
> failed to incorporate planning into the
> chaotic development of our communi-
> ties...
>
> ...The failure to protect and incorpor-
> ate the planning process in our society
> is amply demonstrated by the fact that
> the principal tool of land development
> policy, zoning, is handled in each

---

27. It has been estimated that about half of all cities
that have adopted zoning have no master plans at all. See
Pooley, Planning and Zoning in the United States, at 6
(1961).

> metropolitan area by hundreds of frag-
> mented local governments without cons-
> cious commitment to the concept that
> principles are essential to the estab-
> lishment of meaningful land development
> policies and that rational planning of
> land use must be incorporated in the le-
> gal controls which are adopted to regu-
> late the use of land.[28]

Aside from the fact that planning often lacked a dynamic element, the historical rejection of the planning process in relation to the use of land was due to a number of factors. The principal difficulty was that it delegated to a relatively small group of professionals the task of discovering and weighing, in a supposedly objective manner, the full range of social values attendant to the physical and social development of the community. The underlying assumption is that professionals know enough to predict what the outcomes of the allocative system might be if all values were perfectly represented, an assumption not justified by reality. This can be illustrated by looking at one of the tools advocated for use in planning--cost/benefit analysis--which relies upon a rational approach to decision-making and which, in effect, attempts to simulate the workings of a properly-functioning market. The five step process consists of a definition of objectives in the form of a utility function; enumeration of all possible alternatives actions; the identification of the consequences of such actions; the evaluation of these consequences in terms of objectives via the utility function; and the choice of the action which optimizes utility. Unfortu-

28. Freilich, op. cit. note 24 supra, at 67-68.

nately, there are severe limitations to the application of
such a technique to situations involving impacts on environmental and other "amenity" values associated with
coastal resource allocations. For example, it may be impossible to define all the relevant objectives and their
priorities in developing a utility function; it may be difficult to predict consequences in the presence of uncertainty due to the open nature of the socio-economic system;
and it may be extremely costly and even impossible to perform a comprehensive analysis.   In short, all the factors
which militate against the formation of fully-informed markets for amenity "products" also act to severely impede
methods designed to simulate the market's performance in
this regard. In the case of shoreline resources, we have
noted that this phenomena, which discourages private investment from providing public recreational facilities, applies to government as well, since the values and demands
of a diffuse public may be impossible to identify or too
costly to evaluate.

Given that there is often no easy means of articulating
and weighing the diffuse and intangible values of a diverse
public, there is a danger that allocative decisions will be
determined, by default, by value judgements on the part of
those who administer the planning process.   This, of
course, is one of the risks encountered whenever planning
and decision-making takes place within a basically political arena, where the existence of orderly and efficient
processes for value representation is far less assured than

in the context of the economic marketplace.[29] However, if
master planning begins to rely too heavily on a "father
knows best" approach--as   it often has--it becomes unac-
ceptable in a society such as ours with a strong cultural
bias against any undue centralization of decision-making
authority.

The above observations indicate again the need for new
approaches to any decision-making process, such as coastal
resource management, which necessarily involves substan-
tive interaction between government and community values.
The planning establishment itself has begun to respond to
this need by reevaluating many past concepts and
practices[30] and by experimenting with new and flexible
techniques.[31] The federal government, too, has sought out
new techniques to better incorporate social values into

---

29. This is particularly true when allocative decision-making authority is vested in certain forms of lim-
ited-mandate public agencies, whose actions can often be
shown to lead to resource allocations that are consistently
worse than what an unfettered market would provide, regardless of imperfections.   See, e.g., Ducsik, ed., "The Allocation of Boston Inner Harbor: A Case Study in Resource
Management," Report of the Shoreline Development and Pollution Subcommittee of the Ocean Resources Task Force, at 37,
Massachusetts Secretary of Environmental Affairs (Sept.
1972).

30. The most significant development in relation to the
planning process itself is the American Law Institute's Model Land Development Code, now in its fifth tentative
draft, which represents a major attempt to overhaul the
standard enabling legislation produced during the 1920's.

31. See generally Heeter; Toward a More Effective Land Use
Guidance System; A Summary and Analysis of Five Major Reports, American Society of Planning Officials, Planning Advisory Service Report No. 250 (1969); Freilich, op. cit.
note 24 supra.

agency decision processes, as illustrated by the <u>National Environmental Policy Act of 1969</u>.[32] If collective action is ever to provide a clearly preferable alternative to the market in the allocation of our valuable coastal resources, efforts such as these must continue to be vigorously pursued.

6. Concluding Remarks

I have tried to argue that new modes of collective action are necessary to deal with coastal resources management problems, and that these modes pertain to the interfaces between government and public values, and between different levels and branches within government itself. Finding manageable solutions in the three problem areas outlined herein will obviously be a tall order. What is involved in the "quiet revolution" in resource control is nothing less than an attempt to bring some form of an integral perspective to bear on problems that take place within an extremely decentralized social environment. Whether or not a "counter-revolution" takes place will depend in large measure on the sophistication of the policy techniques that are developed over the next decade or so, and the success they have in dealing with extremely complex issues such as shoreline for the public. The task is grandiose, the techniques are immature, and success is not assured for this goal of developing new and effective management processes

---

32. 42 U.S.C. secs. 4321-4347. NEPA establishes procedural requirements for the preparation of environmental impact statements by federal agencies, thereby laying the groundwork for citizen participation in and judicial review of administration decision processes.

that can prove, in the long run, to be better than the old
ones.

THE COASTAL ZONE MANAGEMENT ACT OF 1972

PUBLIC LAW 92-583, 86 Stat. 1280

An act to establish a national policy and develop a national program for the management, beneficial use, protection, and development of the land and water resources of the Nation's coastal zones, and for other purposes.

Be it enacted by the Senate and House of Representatives of the United States of America in Congress assembled, That the Act entitled "An Act to provide for a comprehensive, long-range, and coordinated national program in marine science, to establish a National Council on Marine Resources and Engineering Development, and a Commission on Marine Science, Engineering and Resources, and for other purposes", approved June 17, 1966 (80 Stat. 203), as amended (33 U.S.C. 1101-1124), is further amended by adding at the end thereof the following new title:

TITLE III--MANAGEMENT OF THE COASTAL ZONE

SHORT TITLE

Sec. 301. This title may be cited as the "Coastal Zone Management Act of 1972".

CONGRESSIONAL FINDINGS

Sec. 302. The Congress finds that--

(a) There is a national interest in the effective management, beneficial use, protection, and development of the coastal zone;

(b) The coastal zone is rich in a variety of natural, commercial, recreational, industrial, and esthetic resources of immediate and potential value to the present and future well-being of the Nation;

(c) The increasing and competing demands upon the lands and waters of our coastal zone occasioned by population growth and economic development, including requirements for industry, commerce, residential development, recreation, ex-traction of mineral resources and fossil fuels, transporta-tion and navigation, waste disposal, and harvesting of fish, shellfish, and other living marine resources, have resulted in the loss of living marine resources, wildlife, nutrient-rich areas, permanent and adverse changes to eco-logical systems, decreasing open space for public use, and shoreline erosion;

(d) The coastal zone, and the fish, shellfish, other living marine resources, and wildlife therein, are ecologi-cally fragile and consequently extremely vulnerable to de-struction by man's alterations:

(e) Important ecological, cultural, historic, and es-thetic values in the coastal zone which are essentïal to the well-being of all citizens are being irretrievably damaged or lost;

(f) Special natural and scenic characteristics are being damaged by ill-planned development that threatens these values;

(g) In light of competing demands and the urgent need to protect and to give high priority to natural systems in the coastal zone, present state and local institutional arrange-ments for planning and regulating land and water uses in such areas are inadequate; and

(h) The key to more effective protection and use of the land and water resources of the coastal zone is to encourage

the states to exercise their full authority over the lands
and waters in the coastal zone by assisting the states, in
cooperation with Federal and local governments and other vi-
tally affected interests, in developing land and water use
programs for the coastal zone, including unified policies,
criteria, standards, methods, and processes for dealing with
land and water use decisions of more than local significance.

DECLARATION OF POLICY

Sec. 303. The Congress finds and declares that it is the
national policy (a) to preserve, protect, develop, and where
possible, to restore or enhance, the resources of the Nation's coastal zone for this and succeeding generations, (b)
to encourage and assist the states to exercise effectively
their responsibilities in the coastal zone through the development and implementation of management programs to
achieve wise use of the land and water resources of the
coastal zone giving full consideration to ecological, cultural, historic, and esthetic values as well as to needs for
economic development, (c) for all Federal agencies engaged
in programs affecting the coastal zone to cooperate and participate with state and local governments and regional agencies in effectuating the purposes of this title, and (d) to
encourage the participation of the public, of Federal,
state, and local governments and of regional agencies in the
development of coastal zone management programs. With respect to implementation of such management programs, it is
the national policy to encourage cooperation among the various state and regional agencies including establishment of
interstate and regional agreements, cooperative procedures,

and joint action particularly regarding environmental problems.

DEFINITIONS

Sec. 304. For the purposes of this title--

(a) "Coastal zone" means the coastal waters (including
the lands therein and thereunder) and the adjacent shorelands (including   the   waters   therein and thereunder),
strongly influenced by each other and in proximity to the
shorelines of the several coastal states, and includes transitional and intertidal areas, salt marshes, wetlands, and
beaches.   The   zone   extends, in Great Lakes waters, to the
international boundary between the United States and Canada
and, in other areas, seaward to the outer limits of the
United States territorial sea. The zone extends inland from
the shorelines only to the extent necessary to control
shorelands, the uses of which have a direct and significant
impact on the coastal waters. Excluded from the coastal
zone are lands the use of which is by law subject solely to
the discretion of or which is held in trust by the Federal
Government, its officers or agents.

(b) "Coastal waters" means (1) in the Great Lakes area,
the waters within the territorial jurisdiction of the United
States consisting of the Great Lakes, their connecting
waters, harbors, roadsteads, and estuary-type areas such as
bays, shallows, and marshes and (2) in other areas, those
waters, adjacent to the shorelines, which contain a measur-
able quantity or percentage of sea water, including, but not
limited to, sounds, bays, lagoons, bayous, ponds, and estuaries.

(c) "Coastal state" means a state of the United States in, or bordering on, the Atlantic, Pacific, or Arctic Ocean, the Gulf of Mexico, Long Island Sound, or one or more of the Great Lakes. For the purposes of this title, the term also includes Puerto Rico, the Virgin Islands, Guam, and American Samoa.

(d) "Estuary" means that part of a river or stream or other body of water having unimpaired connection with the open sea, where the sea water is measurably diluted with fresh water derived from land drainage. The term includes estuary-type areas of the Great Lakes.

(e) "Estuarine sanctuary" means a research area which may include any part or all of an estuary, adjoining transitional areas, and adjacent uplands, constituting to the extent feasible a natural unit, set aside to provide scientists and students the opportunity to examine over a period of time the ecological relationships within the area.

(f) "Secretary" means the Secretary of Commerce.

(g) "Management program" includes, but is not limited to, a comprehensive statement in words, maps, illustrations, or other media of communication, prepared and adopted by the state in accordance with the provisions of this title, setting forth objectives, policies, and standards to guide public and private uses of lands and waters in the coastal zone.

(h) "Water use" means activities which are conducted in or on the water; but does not mean or include the establishment of any water quality standard or criteria or the regulation of the discharge or runoff of water pollutants except the standards, criteria, or regulations which are incorporated in any program as required by the provisions of section 307 (f).

(i) "Land use" means activities which are conducted in or on the shorelands within the coastal zone, subject to the requirements outlined in section 307 (g).

MANAGEMENT PROGRAM DEVELOPMENT GRANTS

Sec. 305. (a) The Secretary is authorized to make annual grants to any coastal state for the purpose of assisting in the development of a management program for the land and water resources of its coastal zone.

(b) Such management program shall include:

(1) an identification of the boundaries of the coastal zone subject to the management program;

(2) a definition of what shall constitute permissible land and water uses within the coastal zone which have a direct and significant impact on the coastal waters;

(3) an inventory and designation of areas of particular concern within the coastal zone;

(4) an identification of the means by which the state proposes to exert control over the land and water uses referred to in paragraph (2) of this subsection, including a listing of relevant constitutional provisions, legislative enactments, regulations, and judicial decisions;

(5) broad guidelines on priority of uses in particular areas, including specifically those uses of lowest priority;

(6) a description of the organizational structure proposed to implement the management program, including the responsibilities and interrelationships of local, areawide, state, regional, and interstate agencies in the management process.

(c) The grants shall not exceed 66 2/3 per centum of the

costs of the program in any one year and no state shall be eligible to receive more than three annual grants pursuant to this section. Federal funds received from other sources shall not be used to match such grants. In order to qualify for grants under this section, the state must reasonably demonstrate to the satisfaction of the Secretary that such grants will be used to develop a management program consistent with the requirements set forth in section 306 of this title. After making the initial grant to a coastal state, no subsequent grant shall be made under this section unless the Secretary finds that the state is satisfactorily developing such management program.

(d) Upon completion of the development of the state's management program, the state shall submit such program to the Secretary for review and approval pursuant to the provisions of section 306 of this title, or such other action as he deems necessary. On final approval of such program by the Secretary, the state's eligibility for further grants under this section shall terminate, and the state shall be eligible for grants under section 306 of this title.

(e) Grants under this section shall be allocated to the states based on rules and regulations promulgated by the Secretary: _Provided, however_, That no management program development grant under this section shall be made in excess of 10 per centum nor less than 1 per centum of the total amount appropriated to carry out the purposes of this section.

(f) Grants or portions thereof not obligated by a state during the fiscal year for which they were first authorized to be obligated by the state, or during the fiscal year immediately following, shall revert to the Secretary, and shall be added by him to the funds available for grants under this section.

(g) With the approval of the Secretary, the state may allocate to a local government, to an areawide agency designated under section 204 of the Demonstration Cities and Metropolitan Development Act of 1966, to a regional agency, or to an interstate agency, a portion of the grant under this section, for the purpose of carrying out the provisions of this section.

(h) The authority to make grants under this section shall expire on June 30, 1977.

ADMINISTRATIVE GRANTS

Sec. 306. (a) The Secretary is authorized to make annual grants to any coastal state for not more than 66 2/3 per centum of the costs of administering the state's management program, if he approves such program in accordance with subsection (c) hereof. Federal funds received from other sources shall not be used to pay the state's share of the costs.

(b) Such grants shall be allocated to the states with approved programs based on rules and regulations promulgated by the Secretary which shall take into account the extent and nature of the shoreline and area covered by the plan, population of the area, and other relevant factors: Provided, however, That no annual administrative grant under this section shall be made in excess of 10 per centum nor less than 1 per centum of the total amount appropriated to carry out the purposes of this section.

(c)   Prior to granting approval of a management program
submitted by a coastal state, the Secretary shall find that:

(1) The state has developed and adopted a management program for its coastal zone in accordance with rules and regulations promulgated by the Secretary, after notice, and with
the opportunity of full participation by relevant Federal
agencies, state agencies, local governments, regional organizations, port authorities, and other interested parties,
public and private, which is adequate to carry out the purposes of this title and is consistent with the policy declared in section 303 of this title.

(2) The state has:

(A) coordinated its program with local, areawide,
and interstate plans applicable to areas within the
coastal zone existing on January 1 of the year in which
the state's management program is submitted to the Secretary, which plans have been developed by a local
government, an areawide agency designated pursuant to
regulations established under section 204 of the Demonstration Cities and Metropolitan Development Act of
1966, a regional agency, or an interstate agency; and

(B) established an effective mechanism for continuing consultation and coordination between the management agency designated pursuant to paragraph (5) of
this subsection and with local governments, interstate
agencies, regional agencies, and areawide agencies
within the coastal zone to assure the full participation of such local governments and agencies in carrying
out the purposes of this title.

(3) The State has held public hearings in the development of the management program.

(4) The management program and any changes thereto have been reviewed and approved by the Governor.

(5) The Governor of the state has designated a single agency to receive and administer the grants for implementing the management program required under paragraph (1) of this subsection.

(6) The state is organized to implement the management program required under paragraph (1) of this subsection.

(7) The state has the authorities necessary to implement the program, including the authority required under subsection (d) of this section.

(8) The management program provides for adequate consideration of the national interest involved in the siting of facilities necessary to meet requirements which are other than local in nature.

(9) The management program makes provision for procedures whereby specific areas may be designated for the purpose of preserving or restoring them for their conservation, recreational, ecological, or esthetic values.

(d) Prior to granting approval of the management program, the Secretary shall find that the state, acting through its chosen agency or agencies, including local governments, areawide agencies designated under section 204 of the Demonstration Cities and Metropolitan Development Act of 1966, regional agencies, or interstate agencies, has authotity for the management of the coastal zone in accordance with the management program. Such authority shall include power--

(1) to administer land and water use regulations, control development in order to ensure compliance with the management program, and to resolve conflicts among competing uses; and

(2) to acquire fee simple and less than fee simple interests in lands, waters, and other property through condemnation or other means when necessary to achieve conformance with the management program.

(e) Prior to granting approval, the Secretary shall also find that the program provides:

(1) for any one or a combination of the following general techniques for control of land and water uses within the coastal zone;

(A) State establishment of criteria and standards for local implementation, subject to administrative review and enforcement of compliance;

(B) Direct state land and water use planning and regulation; or

(C) State administrative review for consistency with the management program of all development plans, projects, or land and water use regulations, including exceptions and variances thereto, proposed by any state or local authority or private developer, with power to approve or disapprove after public notice and an opportunity for hearings.

(2) for a method of assuring that local land and water use regulations within the coastal zone do not unreasonably restrict or exclude land and water uses of regional benefit.

(f) With the approval of the Secretary, a state may allocate to a local government, an areawide agency designated under section 204 of the Demonstration Cities and Metropolitan Development Act of 1966, a regional agency, or an interstate agency, a portion of the grant under this section for the purposes of carrying out the provisions of this section: _Provided,_ That such allocation shall not relieve the state of the responsibility for ensuring that any funds so allocated are applied in furtherance of such state's approved management program.

(g) The state shall be authorized to amend the management program. The modification shall be in accordance with the procedures required under subsection (c) of this section. Any amendment or modification of the program must be approved by the Secretary before additional administrative grants are made to the state under the program as amended.

(h) At the discretion of the state and with the approval of the Secretary, a management program may be developed and adopted in segments so that immediate attention may be devoted to those areas within the coastal zone which most urgently need management programs: _Provided,_ That the state adequately provides for the ultimate coordination of the various segments of the management programs into a single unified program and that the unified program will be completed as soon as is reasonably practicable.

INTERAGENCY COORDINATION AND COOPERATION

Sec. 307. (a) In carrying out his functions and responsibilities under this title, the Secretary shall consult with, cooperate with, and, to the maximum extent practicable, coordinate his activities with other interested Federal agencies.

(b) The Secretary shall not approve the management program submitted by a state pursuant to section 306 unless the views of Federal agencies principally affected by such program have been adequately considered.   In case of serious disagreement between any Federal agency and the state in the

development of the program the Secretary, in cooperation
with the Executive Office of the President, shall seek to
mediate the differences.

(c) (1) Each Federal agency conducting or supporting activities directly affecting the coastal zone shall conduct or
support those activities in a manner which is, to the maximum extent practicable, consistent with approved state management programs.

(2) Any Federal agency which shall undertake any development project in the coastal zone of a state shall insure
that the project is, to the maximum extent practicable, consistent with approved state management programs.

(3) After final approval by the Secretary of a state's
management program, any applicant for a required Federal
license or permit to conduct an activity affecting land or
water uses in the coastal zone of that state shall provide
in the application to the licensing or permitting agency a
certification that the proposed activity complies with the
state's approved program and that such activity will be conducted in a manner consistent with the program. At the same
time, the applicant shall furnish to the state or its designated agency a copy of the certification, with all necessary
information and data. Each coastal state shall establish
procedures for public notice in the case of all such cer-
tifications and, to the extent it deems appropriate, procedures for public hearings in connection therewith. At the
earliest practicable time, the state or its designated agency shall notify the Federal agency concerned that the state
concurs with or objects to the applicant's certification.
If the state or its designated agency fails to furnish the
required notification within six months after receipt of its

copy of the applicant's certification, the state's concurrence with the certification shall be conclusively presumed.
No license or permit shall be granted by the Federal agency
until the state or its designated agency has concurred with
the applicant's certification or until, by the state's failure to act, the concurrence is conclusively presumed, unless
the Secretary, on his own initiative or upon appeal by the
applicant, finds, after providing a reasonable opportunity
for detailed comments from the Federal agency involved and
from the state, that the activity is consistent with the objectives of this title or is otherwise necessary in the interest of national security.

(d) State and local governments submitting applications
for Federal assistance under other Federal programs affecting the coastal zone shall indicate the views of the appropriate state or local agency as to the relationship of such
activities to the approved management program for the
coastal zone. Such applications shall be submitted and coordinated in accordance with the provisions of title IV of
the Intergovernmental Coordination Act of 1968 (82 Stat.
1098). Federal agencies shall not approve proposed projects
that are inconsistent with a coastal state's management program, except upon a finding by the Secretary that such project is consistent with the purposes of this title or necessary in the interest of national security.

(e) Nothing in this title shall be construed--

(1) to diminish either Federal or state jurisdiction,
responsibility, or rights in the field of planning, development, or control of water resources, submerged
lands, or navigable waters; nor to displace, supersede,
limit, or modify any interstate compact or the jurisdic-

tion or responsibility of any legally established joint
or common agency of two or more states and the Federal
Government; nor to limit the authority of Congress to
authorize and fund projects;

(2) as superseding, modifying, or repealing existing
laws applicable to the various Federal agencies; nor to
affect the jurisdiction, powers, prerogatives of the International Joint Commission, United States and Canada,
the Permanent Engineering Board, and the United States
operating entity or entities established pursuant to the
Columbia River Basin Treaty, signed at Washington,
January 17, 1961, or the International Boundary and Water
Commission, United States and Mexico.

(f) Notwithstanding any other provision of this title,
nothing in this title shall in any way affect any requirement (1) established by the Federal Water Pollution Control
Act, as amended, or the Clean Air Act, as amended, or (2)
established by the Federal Government or by any state or local government pursuant to such Acts. Such requirements
shall be incorporated in any program developed pursuant to
this title and shall be the water pollution control and air
pollution control requirements applicable to such program.

(g) When any state's coastal zone management program,
submitted for approval or proposed for modification pursuant
to section 306 of this title, includes requirements as to
shorelands which also would be subject to any Federally supported national land use program which may be hereafter enacted, the Secretary, prior to approving such program, shall
obtain the concurrence of the Secretary of the Interior, or
such other Federal official as may be designated to administer the national land use program, with respect to that

portion of the coastal zone management program affecting such inland areas.

PUBLIC HEARINGS

Sec. 308. All public hearings required under this title must be announced at least thirty days prior to the hearing date. At the time of the announcement, all agency materials pertinent to the hearings, including documents, studies, and other data, must be made available to the public for review and study. As similar materials are subsequently developed, they shall be made available to the public as they become available to the agency.

REVIEW OF PERFORMANCE

Sec. 309. (a) The Secretary shall conduct a continuing review of the management programs of the coastal states and of the performance of each state.

(b) The Secretary shall have the authority to terminate any financial assistance extended under section 306 and to withdraw any unexpended portion of such assistance if (1) he determines that the state is failing to adhere to and is not justified in deviating from the program approved by the Secretary; and (2) the state has been given notice of the proposed termination and withdrawal and given an opportunity to present evidence of adherence or justification for altering its program.

RECORDS

Sec. 310. (a) Each recipient of a grant under this title shall keep such records as the Secretary shall prescribe, including records which fully.disclose the amount and disposition of the funds received under the grant, the total cost of the project or undertaking supplied by other sources, and such other records as will facilitate an effective audit.

(b) The Secretary and the Comptroller General of the United States, or any of their duly authorized representatives, shall have access for the purpose of audit and examination to any books, documents, papers, and records of the recipient of the grant that are pertinent to the determination that funds granted are used in accordance with this title.

ADVISORY COMMITTEE

Sec. 311. (a) The Secretary is authorized and directed to establish a Coastal Zone Management Advisory Committee to advise, consult with, and make recommendations to the Secretary on matters of policy concerning the coastal zone. Such committee shall be composed of not more than fifteen persons designated by the Secretary and shall perform such functions and operate in such a manner as the Secretary may direct. The Secretary shall insure that the committee membership as a group possesses a broad range of experience and knowledge relating to problems involving management, use, conservation, protection, and development of coastal zone resources.

(b) Members of the committee who are not regular full-time employees of the United States, while serving on the business of the committee, including traveltime, may receive compensation at rates not exceeding $100 per diem; and while so serving away from their homes or regular places of business may be allowed travel expenses, including per diem in lieu of subsistence, as authorized by section 5703 of title 5, United States Code, for individuals in the Government service employed intermittently.

ESTUARINE SANCTUARIES

Sec. 312. The Secretary, in accordance with rules and regulations promulgated by him, is authorized to make available to a coastal state grants of up to 50 per centum of the costs of acquisition, development, and operation of estuarine sanctuaries for the purpose of creating natural field laboratories to gather data and make studies of the natural and human processes occurring within the estuaries of the coastal zone. The Federal share of the cost for each such sanctuary shall not exceed $2,000,000. No Federal funds received pursuant to section 305 or section 306 shall be used for the purpose of this section.

ANNUAL REPORT

Sec. 313. (a) The Secretary shall prepare and submit to the President for transmittal to the Congress not later than November 1 of each year a report on the administration of this title for the preceding fiscal year. The report shall include but not be restricted to (1) an identification of the state programs approved pursuant to this title during the preceding Federal fiscal year and a description of those programs; (2) a listing of the states participating in the provisions of this title and a description of the status of each state's programs and its accomplishments during the preceding Federal fiscal year; (3) an itemization of the allocation of funds to the various coastal states and a breakdown of the major projects and areas on which these funds were expended; (4) an identification of any state programs which have been reviewed and disapproved or with respect to which grants have been terminated under this title, and a statement of the reasons for such action; (5) a listing of all activities and projects which, pursuant to the provisions of subsection (c) or subsection (d) of section 307, are not consistent with an applicable approved state management program; (6) a summary of the regulations issued by the Secretary or in effect during the preceding Federal fiscal year; (7) a summary of a coordinated national strategy and program for the Nation's coastal zone including identification and discussion of Federal, regional, state, and local responsibilities and function therein; (8) a summary of outstanding problems arising in the administration of this title in order of priority; and (9) such other information as may be appropriate.

(b) The report required by subsection (a) shall contain such recommendations for additional legislation as the Secretary deems necessary to achieve the objectives of this title and enhance its effective operation.

RULES AND REGULATIONS

Sec. 314. The Secretary shall develop and promulgate, pursuant to section 553 of title 5, United States Code, after notice and opportunity for full participation by relevant Federal agencies, state agencies, local governments, regional organizations, port authorities, and other interested parties, both public and private, such rules and regulations as may be necessary to carry out the provisions of this title.

AUTHORIZATION OF APPROPRIATIONS

Sec. 315. (a) There are authorized to be appropriated--

(1) the sum of $9,000,000 for the fiscal year ending June 30, 1973, and for each of the fiscal years 1974 through 1977 for grants under section 305, to remain available until expended;

(2) such sums, not to exceed $30,000,000, for the fiscal year ending June 30, 1974, and for each of the fiscal years 1975 through 1977, as may be necessary, for grants under section 306 to remain available until expended; and

(3) such sums, not to exceed $6,000,000 for the fiscal year ending June 30, 1974, as may be necessary, for grants under section 312 to remain available until expended.

(b) There are also authorized to be appropriated such sums, not to exceed $3,000,000, for fiscal year 1973 and for each of the four succeeding fiscal years, as may be necessary for administration of this title.

Approved by the 92nd Congress, October 27, 1972.

THE NATIONAL OPEN BEACHES BILL

H.R. 10394

A bill to amend the Act of August 3, 1968, relating to the Nation's estuaries and their natural resources, to establish a national policy with respect to the Nation's beach resources.

Be it enacted by the Senate and House of Representatives of the United States of America in Congress assembled, That the Act entitled "An Act to authorize the Secretary of the Interior, in cooperation with the United States, to conduct an inventory and study of the Nation's estuaries and their natural resources, and for other purposes", approved August 3, 1968 (Public Law 90-454; 82 Stat. 625; 16 U.S.C. 1221 et seq.) is amended as follows:

(1) by inserting immediately after the enacting clause the following:

TITLE I

(2) the first sentence of the first section of such Act is amended by striking out "That" and inserting in lieu thereof "Section 101."

(3) Sections 2 through 6 of such Act are renumbered as sections 102 through 106 respectively, including all references thereto.

(4) by striking out "this Act" each place it appears and inserting in lieu thereof at each such place "this title".

(5) by adding at the end thereof the following new title:

TITLE II

.Sec. 201. As used in this title the term--

(1) 'Secertary' means the Secretary of the Interior.

(2) 'Sea' includes the Atlantic, Pacific, and Arctic Oceans, the Gulf of Mexico, and the Caribbean and Bering Seas, and the Great Lakes.

(3) 'Beach' is the area along the shore of the sea affected by wave action directly from the open sea. It is more precisely defined in the situations and under the conditions hereinafter set forth as follows:

(A) In the case of typically sandy or shell beach with a discernible vegetation line which is constant or intermittent, it is that area which lies seaward from the line of vegetation to the sea.

(B) In the case of a beach having no discernible vegetation line, the beach shall include all area formed by wave action not to exceed two hundred feet in width (measured inland from the point of mean higher high tide).

(4) The 'line of vegetation' is the extreme seaward boundary of natural vegetation which typically spreads continuously inland. It includes the line of vegetation on the seaward side of dunes or mounds of sand typically formed along the line of highest wave action, and, where such a line is clearly defined, the same shall constitute the 'line of vegetation'. In any area where there is no clearly marked vegetation line, recourse shall be had to the nearest marked line of vegetation on each side of such area to determine the elevation reached by the highest waves. The 'line of vegetation' for the unmarked area shall be the line of constant elevation connecting the two clearly marked lines of vegetation on each side. In the event the eleva-

tion of the two points on each side of the area are not the
same, then the extension defining the line reached by the
highest wave shall be the average elevation between the two
points. Such line shall be connected at each of its termini
at the point where it begins to parallel the true vegetation
line by a line connecting it with the true vegetation line
at its farthest extent. Such line shall not be affected by
occasional sprigs of grass seaward from the dunes and shall
not be affected by artificial fill, the addition or removal
of turf, or by other artificial changes in the natural vegetation of the area. Where such changes have been made, and
thus the vegetation line has been obliterated or has been
created artificially, the line of vegetation shall be recon-
structed as it originally exsited, if such is practicable;
otherwise, it shall be determined in the same manner as in
other areas where there is no clearly marked 'line of vegetation,' as in paragraph (3) (B) of this section.

(5) 'Area caused by wave action' means the area to the
point affected by the highest wave of the sea not a storm
wave. It may include scattered stones washed by the sea.

(6) 'Public beaches' are those which, under the provisions of this title, may be protected for use as a common.

(7) 'Matching funds', as provided by a State, include
funds or things of value which may be made available to the
State for the purpose of matching the funds provided by the
Federal Government for purchasing beach easements as, for
instance, areas adjacent to beaches donated by individuals
or associations for the purpose of parking. The value of
such lands or other things used for matching Federal funds
shall be determined by the Secretary. State matching funds
shall not include any moneys which have been supplied
through Federal grants.

(8) 'Shore of the sea' includes those shores on the North American continent, or land adjacent thereto, the State of Hawaii, free commonwealths, unincorporated territories, and trust territories of the United States.

Sec. 202. By reason of their traditional use as a thoroughfare and haven for fishermen and sea ventures, the necessity for them to be free and open in connection with shipping, navigation, salvage, and rescue operations, as well as recreation, Congress declares and affirms that the beaches of the United States are impressed with a national interest and that the public shall have free and unrestricted right to use them as a common to the full extent that such public right may be extended consistent with such property rights of littoral landowners as may be protected absolutely by the Constitution. It is the declared intention of Congress to exercise the full reach of its constitutional power over the subject.

Sec. 203. No person shall create, erect, maintain, or construct any obstruction, barrier, or restraint of any nature which interferes with the free and unrestricted right of the public, individually and collectively, to enter, leave, cross, or use as a common the public beaches.

Sec. 204. (a) An action shall be cognizable in the district courts of the United States without reference to jurisdictional amount, at the instance of the Attorney General or a United States district attorney to:

(1) establish and protect the public right to beaches,

(2) determine the existing status of title, ownership, and control, and

(3) condemn such easement as may reasonably be necessary to accomplish the purposes of this title.

(b) Actions brought under the authority of this section may be for injunctive, declaratory, or other suitable relief.

Sec. 205. The following rules applicable to considering the evidence shall be applicable in all cases brought under section 204 of this title:

(1) a showing that the area is a beach shall be prima facie evidence that the title of the littoral owner does not include the right to prevent the public from using the area as a common;

(2) a showing that the area is a beach shall be prima facie evidence that there has been imposed upon the beach a prescriptive right to use it as a common.

Sec. 206. (a) Nothing in this title shall be held to impair, interfere, or prevent the States--

(1) ownership of its lands and domains,

(2) control of the public beaches in behalf of the public for the protection of the common usage or incidental to the enjoyment thereof, or

(3) authority to perform State public services, including enactment of reasonable zones for wildlife, marine and estuarine protection.

(b) All interests in land recovered under authority of this title shall be treated as subject to the ownership, control and authority of the State in the same measure as if the State itself had acted to recover such interest. In order that such interest be recovered through condemnation, the State must participate in acquiring such interests by providing matching funds of not less than 25 per centum of the value of the land condemned.

Sec. 207. In order further to carry out the purposes of this title, it is desirable that the States and the Federal Government act in a joint partnership to protect the rights and interests of the people in the use of the beaches. The Secretary shall administer the terms and provisions of this title and shall determine what actions shall be brought under Section 204 hereof.

Sec. 208. The Secretary shall place at the disposal of the States such research facilities as may be reasonably available from the Federal Government, and, in cooperation with the other Federal agencies, such other information and facilities as may be reasonably available for assisting the States in carrying out the purposes of this title. The President may promulgate regulations governing the work of such interagency cooperation.

Sec. 209. The Secretary is authorized to make grants to States for carrying out the purposes of this title. Such a grant shall not exceed 75 per centum of the cost of planning, acquisition, or development of projects designed to secure the right of the public to beaches where the State has complied with this title and where adequate State laws are established, in the judgment of the Secretary, to protect the public's right in the beaches.

Sec. 210. The Secretary of Transportation is authorized to provide financial assistance to any State, and to its political subdivisions for the development and maintenance of transportation facilities necessary in connection with the use of public beaches in such State if, in the judgment of the Secretary, such State has defined and sufficiently protected public beaches within its boundaries by State law. Such financial assistance shall be for projects which shall

include, but not be limited to, construction of necessary
highways and roads to give access to the shoreline area,
the construction of parking lots and adjacent park areas,
as well as related transportation facilities. All sums appropriated to carry out title 23 of the United States Code
are authorized to be made available to carry out this section.

———————————

Introduced by Rep. Robert Eckhardt on September 19, 1973,
and referred to the Committee on Merchant Marine and Fisheries. Companion legislation (S.2621) was introduced in
the Senate by Sentor Henry Jackson on October 30, 1973.

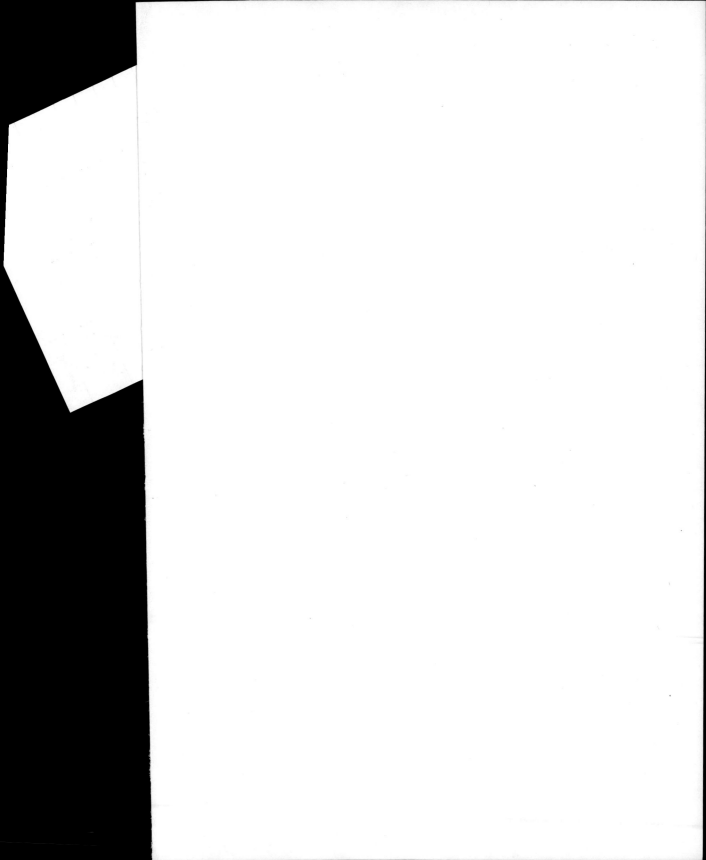